North East India

SELECTED REGIONAL ISSUES

North East India

SELECTED REGIONAL ISSUES

Edited by

Prof. Amar Yumnam

Manipur University, Imphal
Manipur

•

AKANSHA PUBLISHING HOUSE
NEW DELHI • GUWAHATI • VISAKHAPATNAM

AKANSHA PUBLISHING HOUSE
4649-B/21, Ansari Road
Darya Ganj, New Delhi - 110 002
Ph.: 23263193 / 9811582579 / 09435116718
Fax: 011-23263193
Email: ektabooks@yahoo.com
www.akanshapublishinghouse.com

North East India: Selected Regional Issues

First Published 2011
ISBN 978-81-8370-308-6
Reprint - 2021

Advisory Committee

1. Professor E. Bijoykumar Singh – Head, Department of Economics– Member
2. Professor S. Dorendrajit Singh – Head, Department of Physics– Member
3. Professor N. Deva Singh – Head, Department of Geography– Member
4. Professor Amar Yumnam – Dean, School of Social Sciences– Chairman

PRINTED IN INDIA

Published by Akansha Publishing House, New Delhi for Manipur University, Imphal and Printed at Harmain Offset Press, Delhi.

Contents

Preface

The Academic Council of Manipur University decided in its wisdom that the Undergraduate students of the university should be made aware of some of the significant contemporary aspects of the Society, Polity and Economy of North East Region of India (NER) in general and Manipur in particular. This book is in response to the mandate of the university.

The Advisory Committee decided on five key aspects for concentration. They are:

a. Economic Development;
b. Demography;
c. History and Polity;
d. Culture; and
e. Women.

The contributors to the book have been guided by the principle of exposing the students to the key concepts relevant to the fields covered while making them appreciate the basic issues prevailing in the region. The first has the objective of arousing the specialisation interests of the students in order to help them in choosing their future fields while the latter aims at enabling them to situate in the region. In other words, the expositions in the various chapters centre on the core concepts of the relevant fields.

Chapter 1 in this book deals with the development trajectory of the NER. This chapter would give the student a flavour of how economists go about analysing development issues. It would also give an idea on the use of indicators to situate a region in the development map.

Population is an important resource in any society. So how it evolves over time and interacts with the development process are important aspects an intelligent person should be conversant with. Chapter 2 addresses these issues in the context of the region.

Culture is an issue very close to the hearts of the people of the region. It is a result of dynamics of cumulative interaction across different groups of people in any heterogeneous population. Besides it can be understood in the context of the environment in which the population survives. Chapter 3 gives an idea on how this has evolved in Manipur over the centuries.

Understanding a society is never complete without an idea of her history and polity. Chapter 4 has the objective of making the students aware of the historical background and the prevailing political structure of Manipur. After reading this chapter, the student would be fairly conversant with the historical background and contemporary political structure of Manipur.

Anything relating to women are very sensitive issues in the region, and particularly so in Manipur. Women here are considered to be enjoying a kind of status and existence unique to the region. In fact, an understanding of the region would be incomplete without an analysis of the women issues as experienced here. The last chapter provides an appreciation of these issues in a larger framework.

It is hoped that the students would be better knowledgeable about their world after studying the five chapters in this book. As Editor, I would like to put on record the appreciation of the University the efforts of the contributors for their wonderful work within a very short span of time.

Editor

Our Contributors

1. **Amar Yumnam** – Professor of Economics, Manipur University. Specialises in Development Economics with Institutional Economics and New Economic Geography as current areas of interest.
2. **E. Bijoykumar Singh** – Professor of Economics, Manipur University. Specialises in Mathematical Economics and Econometrics.
3. **M. C. Arun** – Associate Professor in Anthropology, Manipur University. Specialises in social and cultural anthropology.
4. **M. Hemanta Meitei** – Reader in Economics, Manipur University. Specialises in Demography.
5. **N. Deva Singh** – Professor of Geography, Manipur University.
6. **N. Joykumar Singh** – Professor in History, Manipur University. Specialises in modern Indian and Regional history.
7. **N. Vijaylakshmi Brara** – Reader in the Centre for Manipur Studies, Manipur University. Specialises in research on culture and gender issues.
8. **S. Mangi Singh** – Professor in Political Science, Manipur University. Specialises in Indian political system and State politics.
9. **Seromena Asem** – Lecturer in Liberal College, Manipur. Specialises in research on gender issues.

1

Economic Development of North Eastern Region of India

—E. Bijoykumar Singh & Amar Yumnam

The North Eastern Region (NER) comprises of Arunachal Pradesh, Assam, Manipur, Meghalaya, Mizoram, Nagaland, Sikkim and Tripura and extends to north and east of the narrow Siliguri corridor. These eight States cover an area of 2,63,179 sq. km. constituting 8 per cent of the country's total geographical area and account for only around 3.76 per cent of the total population and 3.87 per cent of country's output.[1] The region shares a long international boundary with China and Bhutan in the north, Myanmar in the east, Nepal in the west and Bangladesh in the south and west. In fact, almost 4,500 kilometres or 98 per cent the boundary of the NER are

---

[1]While population refers to the year 2011, and output refers to Net State Domestic Product (NSDP) of the year 2008-09, taken at constant prices with base 1990-2000=100, sourced from RBI. Constant prices of a base year make the comparison of output or income over a period of time meaningfully possible. All the other prices of subsequent (in some cases previous) years are converted into prices of this base year.

international borders. The mostly mountainous[2] States in the region like Arunachal Pradesh, Meghalaya, Mizoram and Nagaland are inhabited mainly by tribal population as defined in the Indian Constitution. The region has over 200 of the 635 tribal groups in the country speaking a variety of Tibeto-Burman languages and dialects with a strong tradition of social and cultural identity. Rich in natural resources and a treasure house of floral and faunal bio–diversity, the region was a gateway to East and Southeast Asia before independence. Today this region has come to be considered a backward region having been bypassed by the process of development. History, geography and politics have combined to cast the region as a far away land, remote, isolated and surrounded by intimidating and hostile environment. The politico-social tensions which have characterised this region for quite a few years by now are also attributed to the lack or quality of development, while at the same time coupling the challenges of development.

---

[2] After the Year of the Mountains in 2002, this term is now used more for academic purposes than the usual 'mountain'. We follow the United Nations Environment Program – World Conservation Monitoring Centre definition of mountains as a land mass with slope and/or elevation; this definition encompasses mountains as well as distinct from conventional understanding. The current classifications are: Class 1- elevation of 4,500 meters and above; Class 2 - elevation of 3,500–4,500 meters; Class 3 - elevation of 2,500–3,500 meters; Class 4 - elevation of 1,500–2,500 meters and slope; Class 5 - elevation of 1,000–1,500 meters and slope, or local elevation range of 7 kilometer radius- 300 meters; Class 6- elevation of 300–1,000 meters and local elevation range of 7 kilometer radius - 300 meters outside 23⁰N—19⁰ S; and Class 7 - isolated inner basins and plateaus less than 25 square kilometers in extent that are surrounded by mountains but do not themselves meet criteria 1–6 (this seventh class was introduced in the 2002 revision of the original 2000 system). UNEP-WCMC (World Conservation Monitoring Centre), 2002: *Mountain Watch: environmental change and sustainable development in mountains.* Cambridge, UK.

This essay tries to examine the following issues:

(i) What do we understand by economic development?

(ii) What has been the status of development in this region?

(iii) What strategies should be adopted to streamline the process of development in this region?

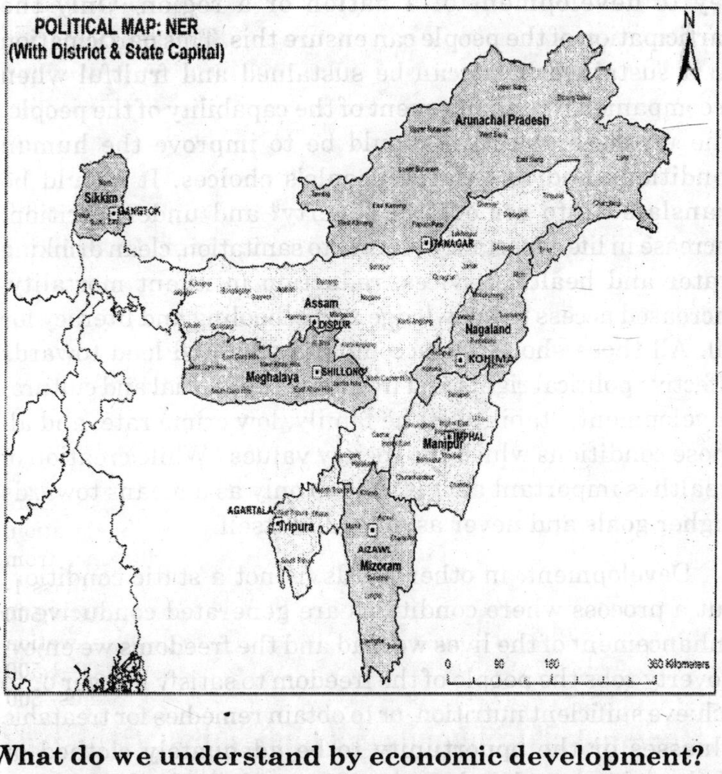

What do we understand by economic development?

Economic development is the undisputed objective of any society. However the scope of the concept has evolved and is still evolving as we come to understand more and more of what makes our lives complete. Today it means a sustained increase in income accompanied by a general rise in the well being and economic capabilities of people, given geography (climate, disease conditions, and topography, etc.) and the institutions (social norms, structure of law, and property rights, etc). In the process of development the nature of geography and the institutions themselves have to undergo changes both as a result and a prelude to further development. Proper utilisation of natural (geographical asset) and cultural (institutional asset) resources holds the key to development of a nation or a region. Only the participation of the people can ensure this. This participation on a sustained basis can be sustained and fruitful when accompanied by enhancement of the capability of the people. The ultimate objective should be to improve the human conditions and to enlarge people's choices. It should be translated into removal of poverty[3] and undernutrition, increase in life expectancy[4], access to sanitation, clean drinking water and health services, reduction in infant mortality, increased access to knowledge and schooling and literacy for all. All these should be accompanied by and lead towards effective political rights and freedom, intellectual and cultural development, stability of the family, low crime rate, and all those conditions which the society values. While creation of wealth is important as it is, it is so only as a means towards higher goals and never as an end in itself.

Development, in other words, is not a static condition, but a process where conditions are generated conducive to enhancement of the lives we lead and the freedoms we enjoy. Poverty robs the people of the freedom to satisfy hunger or to achieve sufficient nutrition, or to obtain remedies for treatable illnesses or the opportunity to be adequately clothed or sheltered or to enjoy clean water or sanitary facilities. Such

---

[3] Poverty is deprivation of the basic human needs.

[4] Life expectancy at birth is the average number of years a newly born child will live if he is subjected to the current age specific mortality rates.

lack of freedom is closely associated with the lack of government-provided public facilities and social care such as the absence of epidemiological programmes or of organised arrangements for health care or educational facilities or of effective institutions for the maintenance of local peace and order. When we talk about a developed country, we think of a society where the people are well fed and well clothed, enjoy access to a variety of commodities, have the luxury of some leisure and entertainment and live in a healthy environment. A minimal requirement of life in a developed nation is that the physical quality of an individual be high and be so uniformly, rather than being restricted to an affluent minority.

What has been the status of development in this region?

Development is usually measured through indicators like literacy rate[5], infant mortality rates[6], poverty ratio[7], real per capita NSDP[8], per capita electricity consumption and road length in kilometre per 1000 sq. km of geographical area. Rise in literacy rate, real per capita NSDP, per capita electricity consumption and road length in km. per 1000 sq. km of geographical area is highly desirable while fall in infant mortality rate and poverty ratio is to be targeted. It can also be measured by aggregated measures such as human development index where three dimensions of development–standard of living, knowledge and health – constitute an index.[9]

---

[5] Literacy rate is the percentage of people above age seven years who can read and write with understanding.

[6] Infant mortality rate is the number of infants per 1000 live births who die before the age of one year.

[7] Poverty ratio is the percentage of people unable to meet the national minimum requirements for not to be deemed poor.

[8] Real per capita NSDP stands for state income measured in constant prices.

[9] Indices of development are still being researched upon and developed.

Sex Ratio

Sex ratio is an indicator of the status of women in the society. Only three states have a sub-national sex ratio. Sex ratio in the region rose from 937 to 956 during 2001-2011. North eastern states are not known for widespread discrimination against females as in many other parts of India. The Khasis in Meghalaya follow a matriarchal system where women inherit the property of parents. Urban population enjoy facilities not accessible to rural population.[10] Higher is the level of development, higher will be the extent of urbanisation. NER is basically a rural economy; almost 84 per cent of population live in rural areas, having an average population density of 173 people per sq. km. of area *(Table 1.1)*. The distribution of population is also uneven across the states. Assam and Tripura are top two densely populated states, sharing almost 76.4 per cent of total NER population. Assam alone has 68.4 per cent. Among the 28 states Meghalaya had the highest decadal growth of population at 27.82 per cent and Nagaland had the distinction of being the only state with a negative decadal growth rate at (-)0.47. During 1991-2001 only two states i.e. Assam and Tripura had a decadal growth rate lower than the national growth rate and during 2001-11 the number rose to four i.e. Assam, Tripura, Sikkim and Nagaland.

---

[10] Urban: In the Census of India 2001, the definition of urban area adopted is as follows: (a) All statutory places with a municipality, corporation, cantonment board or notified town area committee, etc. (b) A place satisfying the following three criteria simultaneously:

i) a minimum population of 5,000; ii) at least 75 per cent of male working population engaged in non-agricultural pursuits; and iii) a density of population of at least 400 per sq. km. (1,000 per sq. mile).

Table 1.1
Population by NER States (2011 Census)

NER States	*Total*	*Sex ratio (females per 1000 males)*	*Urban* (%)*	*Pop Density (per sq. km area)*
Arunachal Pradesh	1382611	920	20.75	17
Assam	31169272	954	12.90	397
Manipur	2721756	987	26.28	122
Meghalaya	2964007	986	19.58	132
Mizoram	1091014	975	49.63	52
Nagaland	1980602	931	17.23	119
Sikkim	607688	889	11.07	86
Tripura	3671032	961	17.06	350
NER Total	45587982	956	15.66	173
All states	1,21,01,93,422	940	27.82	382

*Share in total population for 2001.
Source: Census of India 2011 provisional population totals.

Net State Domestic Product

The standard of living of the people in the region, as measured by per capita Net State Domestic Product (NSDP), has lagged significantly behind the rest of the country (Table 1.2). Interestingly, available information shows that at the time of independence per capita income in the undivided State of Assam was higher than the national average by 4 per cent.[11] Thus, even under the British colonial rule the economic performance of the region was better than the rest of the country and this shows its vast developmental potential. The

[11] At the time of Independence NER consisted of Assam, Manipur and Tripura.

slow progress of NER's economy is reflected in the low growth in income. As the growth rate of per capita GSDP lagged behind the rest of the country the gap narrowed, and by the late 1960s per capita income in the region had fallen behind. However, over time, differences in the growth rates in per capita income between the region and the country increased further. During the period 1999-00 to 2008-09, on an average, while the Indian economy in constant prices grew at the rate of 7.2 per cent per year, the corresponding growth in the NER region was 6.67 per cent. Similarly, the region's growth rate of per capita income also lagged behind the national growth rate of the country. Not surprisingly, the difference in per capita incomes between the country and the region has steadily diverged. In 1999-2000 only Mizoram had a per capita NSDP higher than the all India figure and by 2008-9 there was no such State in the region. The per capita NSDP of NER declined from being 89.29% of all India per capita NNP to 79.09% over the period.

Table 1.2

Comparative Profile of per capita real NSDP

State	*1999-2000*	*Latest figure*	*Reference year of Latest figure*
Arunachal Pradesh	13990	22475	2008-9
Assam	12282	17080	2009-10
Manipur	13260	16508	2008-9
Meghalaya	14355	23069	2008-9
Mizoram	16443	19750	2007-8
Nagaland	14107	17129	2006-7
Sikkim	14890	25257	2008-9
Tripura	14119	22493	2007-8
NER	14181	20470	
All India per capita NNP	15881	25881	2008-9

Source: RBI (2009-10) *Handbook of Statistics on the Indian Economy.*

Other Indicators

The region lags behind the rest of the country not only in

terms of per capita income but in several other development indicators as well (Table 1.3). People do not have access to basic services in adequate measure. The standard development indicators such as road length, access to healthcare, and power consumption in the region are below the national averages. The region's per capita power consumption of power at 110 kwh is almost a fourth of the national average (411 kwh). In Assam, Manipur and Nagaland, the per capita power consumption is as low as 85 kwh, 70 kwh and 87 kwh, respectively. The literacy rate in the region is high, but the slow pace of industrialisation and limited capacity of the population to engage in productive economic activities means a high rate of unemployment and underemployment. The incidence of poverty in the region is high except for Meghalaya, Mizoram and Nagaland.

Table 1.3

Various indicators of NER states

State	*Literacy Rate 2011 (%)*	*Infant Mortality Rate (per1000) 2004-5*	*Poverty Ratio (2004-05) Tendulkar Report*	*Per Capita Electricity Consumption (Kwh) 2004-5*	*Road length (km/'000 sqkm of geographical area (2008)*
Arunachal Pradesh	66.95	61	31.1	144.8	196.96
Assam	73.18	66	34.4	35.3	2936.51
Manipur	79.85	30	38.0	70.05	739.11
Meghalaya	75.48	45	16.1	352.2	438.57
Mizoram	91.58	34	15.3	133.7	292.11
Nagaland	80.11	38	9.0	87.2	1345.32
Sikkim	82.20	34	31.1	397.7	263.95
Tripura	87.75	52	40.6	113.1	3026.23
NER	74.58	45		110.4	
All states	74.04	57	37.2	411.1	965.73

Notes: Poverty ratio: Tendulkar Report; Road length: Statistical Handbook of India 2010 RBI.

Economic Structure

By structure of an economy we mean the relative importance of different sectors. Broadly speaking an economy has the following categorisations:

- *Agriculture & allied sector:* agriculture, forestry and logging, fishing
- *Industry:* Mining and quarrying, manufacturing, electricity, gas and water supply
- *Services:* construction, transport, storage & communication, trade, hotels and restaurants, banking & insurance, real estate, ownership of dwelling & business, public administration, other services.

Modern economic growth has been accompanied with a change in the structure of the economy whereby the importance of agriculture gradually declined and that of industry gradually increasing. Ultimately the share of the service sector also will rise. A structural change in short means a perpetual rise of the share of industry and non-farm outputs in the gross domestic product over time. A rapid structural change is always associated with the economic growth of any region. Various countries including India have undergone this structural change.

Within the region (Table 1.4), except for Nagaland, the share of agriculture has declined during 1999-2000 and 2008-9. The share of services has increased except in Meghalaya and Nagaland. Unfortunately, the share of industry in the NSDP of NER has been only 10 per cent in 2008-09, remaining where it was in 1999-2000. The share varies across the States and has been lower than the all India share. This indicates the failure of the industrialization process to take off in the region. The poor performance of the industrial sector seems to be one of the prime causes of the relatively poor performance of NSDP growth of the region.

Table 1.4
Structural change in NER
(percentage of real NSDP)

State	*1999-2000*			*2008-9*		
	Agri-culture	*Indu-stry*	*Services*	*Agri-culture*	*Indu-stry*	*Services*
Arunachal Pradesh	36	5	59	25	7	68
Assam	36	11	53	26	12	62
Manipur	31	9	60	23	8	69
Meghalaya	24	11	65	20	16	64
Mizoram	21	4	75	16	4	80
Nagaland	33	2	65	34	3	63
Sikkim	23	9	68	18	7	75
Tripura	26	6	68	24	5	71
NER	33	10	57	25	10	65
All India*	25	20	55	15	20	65

**Share of GDP, 2009-10 with 2004-5 as base.*

Table 1.5 shows how important the primary sector has been across the States in terms of its share in the workforce. The declining contribution in NSDP and stagnant share of workforce indicate a falling labour productivity in agriculture. Agricultural growth has been uneven across regions and crops. NER continues to be a net importer of foodgrains. In spite of covering 8.8 per cent of the country's total geographical area, NER produces only 1.5 per cent of the country's total foodgrain production.

Table 1.5
Sectoral Distribution of Workers (2001)

State	*Rural*			*Urban*		
	Primary	*Secon-dary*	*Tertiary*	*Primary*	*Secon-dary*	*Tertiary*
Arunachal Pradesh	83.4	7.5	9	8.7	13.4	77.9
Assam	67.7	6.2	26.2	6	13.5	80.5
Manipur	75.3	8.9	15.8	28.3	15.6	55.9
Meghalaya	86.5	3	10.5	1.3	14.6	84.1
Mizoram	88.5	2.4	12.2	30.3	14.7	55
Nagaland	79.7	2.2	18.1	8.4	12.1	79.5
Sikkim	60.8	9.9	29.3	2.1	16.1	81.8
Tripura	45.7	12	42.3	2.7	8	89.3
India	76.3	11.4	12.4	8.8	32	59.2

Source: Census of India 2001

Except for Arunachal Pradesh and Manipur, the main source of growth in income is tertiary sector (Table 1.6). In Mizoram the contribution of tertiary sector is exceedingly high.[12] In Manipur and Arunachal Pradesh the main source of growth is the secondary sector. In none of the States is the primary sector the main source of growth though it contributes a significant proportion in Arunachal Pradesh, Assam and Sikkim. It shows the growing role of the non-commodity producing sector in the growth of the economy. It should be noted that public administration is an important sub-sector of the tertiary sector and it is not related with commodity production as directly as the activities in primary and secondary sector.

[12] Tertiary sector is services without construction sub-sector. Secondary sector is industry with construction and without mining and quarrying. Primary sector is agriculture and allied with mining and quarrying.

Table 1.6
Contribution of Sectors to Growth of NSDP (in percent) 1980-81 to 2006-7 (at 1980-1 prices)

State	*Average annual growth rate*	*Contribution of*		
		Primary	*Secondary*	*Tertiary*
Arunachal Pradesh	7.956	32.6	36.0	31.4
Assam	3.328	30.81	16.78	52.41
Manipur	5.510	18.42	45.61	35.97
Meghalaya	5.197	21.09	13.76	63.15
Mizoram	6.018	2.0	21.38	76.62
Nagaland	6.8976	26.35	19.81	53.84
Tripura	6.253	18.91	19.33	61.76
Sikkim	8.851	33.88	29.93	36.19

Rural Economy

The progress of rural economy is the sine-qua-non for development of NER. This is mainly for two reasons. Firstly, over 80 per cent of the population of the region lives in rural areas and its livelihood depends on agricultural and allied activities.[13] Secondly, there is abundance of natural resources in the economy and harnessing these for the benefit of the population would require strengthening forward and backward linkages.[14] Development of rural economies in the region may rest on activities like agriculture, forestry, livestock, minerals and rural non-farm activity. The falling share of primary sector in income generation along with the high share in rural employment indicates falling productivity

[13] Rural -urban data for 2011 are not yet available.

[14] Linkages are the relationships among different economic activities either in consumption or production.

Table 1.7

Household Amenities in NER States (as percentage of respective totals)

State	*PH (2001)*	*SW (2001)*	*PCe (1999-2000) Kwh*	*Hec (2001)*	*Deprivation Index (2001)*		*Urban population (2001)*
					Rural	*Urban*	
Arunachal Pradesh	20.68	77.5	95.5	54.7	41.54	18.15	20.4
Assam	19.47	58.8	95.5	24.9	43.59	18.47	12.7
Manipur	8.39	37.0	69.5	60.0	39.22	23.18	23.9
Meghalaya	22.14	39.0	160.3	42.7	49.55	16.50	19.6
Mizoram	52.84	36.0	120.8	69.6	42.55	19.43	49.5
Nagaland	16.19	46.5	84.7	63.6	40.92	18.96	17.7
Sikkim	37.87	70.7	192.4	77.8	37.7	4.93	11.1
Tripura	9.81	52.5	95.5	41.8	40.3	17.43	17.0
India	51.62	77.9	354.7	55.9	45.74	16.79	27.8

Note: PH pucca housing; SW access to safe drinking water; PCe per capita consumption of electricity in kwh; Hec Household with electricity connection; DI deprivation index; UP urban population.

Source: Census 2001.

in this sector. The benefits of growth accrue largely to the small portion of workers in the tertiary sector. This will worsen the income inequality scenario in the region.

Household amenities such as pucca housing, access to safe drinking water, per capita consumption of electricity and the extent of urbanisation indicate the quality of life. The proportion of pucca houses in the region is much lower than the all India level, except for Mizoram. The per capita consumption of electricity is uniformly low in all the States in the region. Deprivation index[15] of rural areas is much higher than that of urban area. The low level of urbanisation and relatively higher deprivation index of rural areas indicate the low overall quality of life.

Unemployment

Youth unemployment rate (Table 1.8) in urban areas is quite high, with most of the States having a much higher unemployment rate than the all India rate. This is in sharp contrast with the overall unemployment rates which are much lower than the all India rate. Low rural unemployment rate need not necessarily mean abundant work opportunities in rural areas. It may be attributed to the inability of the rural labour force to remain unemployed for long because of their poverty.

Human Development Index

Does a low growth rate or a declining growth rate of various aggregates doom the people of the region in an unenviable position? Not necessarily so because Table 1.9 shows that in terms of the more encompassing measure of development popularly known as *human development index* the States in the region have been doing quite well. In 1981

[15] It is a non-income measure of poverty derived from *a measure that aggregates data on the prevalence of different types of deprivation,*

Manipur's rank was fourth, and in 1991 Mizoram was the 7th ranked Indian State. In 2005 also seven States had HDI higher than that of all India and Mizoram's rank rose to 4th. Thus the income gap has been made up by better performance in education and health. This indicates the strength of social capital[16] which needs to be nurtured to attain higher level, by not insisting on mainstreaming uncritically. The problem arises when we try to impose on others what we consider to be good for them without regard to how they themselves feel about it. If some amount of growth has to be sacrificed to develop the social capital that may be more productive in the long run. After all nation-building is not a short term exercise.

Table 1.8

Youth Unemployment Rate (2004-05)

(usual principal status)

State	*Rural*			*Urban*		
	Male	*Female*	*Total*	*Male*	*Female*	*Total*
Arunachal Pradesh	3	1.7	2.5	5.6	7.4	4
Assam	8.5	15.3	9.7	20.9	33.4	23.3
Manipur	5.1	2.3	3.9	19.7	18.5	19.3
Meghalaya	0.2	1.6	0.8	12.9	12	12.5
Mizoram	2	0.3	1.3	4.4	6.2	4.9
Nagaland	20.8	9.5	14.9	22.1	35.5	27.7
Sikkim	8.6	4	7	6.7	6.3	8
Tripura	25.7	60.8	33	45.4	83.7	61.4
India	5.2	7	5.7	10	19.9	11.9

Source: NSSO(2006) "Employment and Unemployment Situation in India 2004-05" Report no.515

[16] Social capital is an encompassing term that connotes the arrangements and support systems embedded in a society that make social and cultural life possible. The most emphasized feature is the level of trust prevailing in a society.

Table 1.9
Human Development Index of North Eastern States (1981-2005)

State	*1981*	*1991*	*2005**
Arunachal Pradesh	0.242(31)	0.328(29)	0.617(22)
Assam	0.272(26)	0.348(26)	0.534(29)
Manipur	0.481(4)	0.536(9)	0.707(11)
Meghalaya	0.317(21)	0.365(24)	0.585(26)
Mizoram	0.411(8)	0.548(7)	0.790(4)
Nagaland	0.328(20)	0.486(11)	0.770(7)
Sikkim	0.342(18)	0.425(18)	0.684(13)
Tripura	0.287(24)	0. 389(22)	0.608(23)
All India	0.302	0.381	0.575

Source: Human Development Report 2001, Planning Commission
*The HDI's in 2005 are from Meghalaya HDR (2008)

Note: Figures in parentheses are all India ranks.

The policies

The discussion on the appropriate policy initiatives will be more meaningful when it is framed against the backdrop of the reasons behind the current state of affairs and the vision of the people.

Causes of Underdevelopment

The major factors constraining the economic development of this region are *initial conditions*, *infrastructure deficiency*, *insurgency*, *imperfection / distortion in factor* and *product markets* and *indifferent governance.*[17]

---

[17] The debate on the causes continues. The arguments put forward by Prof. Atul Sarma accommodated almost all viewpoints and hence have been used as the framework in this essay.

1. Initial conditions

(i) *Disruption of traditional links:* Driven by expanding global trade and investment and triggered by innovations, the 'region was in the forefront of development almost 150 years ago. The expanding global trade was conducted through the sea route through Chittagong, network of inland waterways, and land transportation through road and railways. In fact, the railway network between Dibrugarh and Chittagong was one of the earliest projects in India implemented by the British in the late 19th century. If the road to the north from Gangtok established the 'Silk Route' for trade with China, the port town of Chittagong served as the gateway for global trade. The large river systems and small rivulets provided a means of livelihood for the vast majority of the population in the valleys and plains. The natural transportation route through East Bengal not merely reduced the physical distance but brought emotional closeness as well to make Manipur to participate in the independence movement.[18] The rapid spread of tea gardens following the first garden in 1835 and the export of the first consignment of tea to London in 1838 ensured employment and prosperity to the people of Assam. The discovery of oil in Makum pathar and establishment of a crude oil refinery in Digboi in 1890 laid the foundation for the development of undivided Assam. The zeal of the missionaries was largely responsible for spreading literacy. Partition disrupted the continuity of the process. *The distance between Kolkata and Agartala was 300 km in pre- partition era and it rose to 1700 km in post-partition era.* Sarma says that " ... in pre-partition days, boats laden with tea, coal and timber reached Kolkata from Dibrugarh in 8 days. But now from Kolkata to Guwahati it

[18] The first generation of educated Manipuris was educated in Sylhet, now in Bangladesh. Bengali literature also had profound influence on Manipuri literature.

takes more than 25 days for lack of night navigation and customs formalities at various points." The considerable market disruption, socioeconomic distancing and retardation that resulted due to partition are yet to be compensated.

(ii) *Population influx form across the borders:* the influx of population that had started since partition continues to remain a cause of social and political mobilisation leading to a prolonged disturbed situation unfriendly for investment and growth.

(iii) *Unharnessed resource endowments:* Hydropower potential as well as oil and gas based downstream industries remain undeveloped. Water resources have continued to cause flood and erosion year after year resulting in immense human sufferings and loss of lives. Such regular devastation of farmland weakened farmers' incentives for investment.

(iv) *Enclave economy:* Crude oil production and its refining, plantation and plywood industry are few resources based modern industries in the region. But oil and tea industries have not induced any industrial growth based on their backward and forward linkages. The backward linkage based industries of tea industry i.e. fertilizers, insecticides, chappals, umbrelas, small tools, etc. are coming from outside the region. The oil industry also was not accompanied with petrochemical complexes. The modern industries remained enclave economies without any linkage with the larger segment of traditional activities.

(v) *Monopolistic operations of deeply entrenched trading interests:* The region gets its requirement though trade and distribution network. Foodgrains, edible oil, fish, etc. are imported. The trade network is organised on the basis of monopolistic competition.[19] Entrenched mercantile capital prevents the emergence of local entrepreneurship. Shukla Commission, which looked into the development needs of the region, estimated that about Rs 2,500 crore worth of consumables are imported from outside the region every year. The banking sector transfers about Rs 5000 crores from this region to other regions for investment. NER is a growing market of nearly 50 million people where most of the requirements are still being 'imported' from other parts of India, rather than being produced in the region itself. The business of 'import' and distribution across the region has led to the emergence and strengthening of interest groups. These interest groups in league with 'uninterested' bureaucracy see to it that the incentives for entrepreneurship never reach the entrepreneurs in any meaningful manner. There are innumerable cases of local entrepreneurs outcompeted in the market by bigger entrepreneurs.[20]

2. Infrastructure deficiency

The region lacks the basic minimum physical, social and administrative infrastructures for growth. Physical infrastructure such as power, communications, transports, irrigation and market access are grossly inadequate. Poor infrastructure is not conducive to attracting private investment. Although the NER is rich in resources like hydrocarbons, forest, hydro-electricity, and other minerals, high transportation cost did not allow her to grow according to her comparative advantages. The high transportation cost coupled with the higher level of prices and low level of investment have worked as a double squeeze on the well being of the people in this region. The connectivity

[19] Monopolistic competition is a kind of market where different sellers offer similar but not identical products, thus giving them a scope to set prices of their products.

[20] Though 'survival of the fittest' is the market norm, the repeated episodes of abortion of industrial impulses have been given various interpretations. The destruction of nascent industries producing polythene carry-bags, candles, car batteries in post border-trade Manipur since 1995 is a glaring example.

bottlenecks have made the region perpetually underdeveloped and hence politically volatile.

3. Insurgency

Insurgency is associated with high transaction cost. Most of the insurgencies had their origin in underdevelopment. Insurgency has been listed as both effect and cause of underdevelopment of this region. This has become an excuse for the rent seeking behaviour of bureaucrats and politicians. Substantial amount of money earmarked for developmental projects have leaked to the insurgents. Except for Sikkim which became a part of India in 1975, there is no State in this region which has not passed through different phases of insurgency. Not only have funds for developmental projects been diverted, but an increasing amount of money, which could have been earmarked for developmental projects, are also being spent on maintenance of law and order. The conflicts in some of the States can be termed low intensity wars.

4. Distortions in factor and commodity markets

Large inflow of goods and outflow of savings impede growth. Due to low production base and heavy dependence on the rest of the country for their requirements, growth of local demand induces income and employment generation in the States with larger production base outside the region. Low credit deposit ratio implies most of the deposits in the region being invested outside the region.

5. Indifferent governance[21]

The State governments in the region have not contributed

---

[21] Governance is the process of making decisions and implementing or non-implementing decisions to achieve stated objectives. While the concept can be applied to both formal and informal and also government and non-governmental agencies, the critical aspect of this in the region applies to the character of the state as manifested in the governance functioning of the region.

much in mainstreaming the development process. Except for Tripura and Sikkim, other States in the region have a poor governance record. Many opportunities have thus been squandered.

Consistent pursuit of clearly defined priorities with a development perspective contributes to growth. While development can benefit from good luck, in all cases be achieved in a sustainable way in the absence of well articulated thrusts pursued over a period of time.

In the beginning the development initiatives in the region used to be anchored on two perspectives: security perspective and perspective based on least interference in traditional institutions and practices. Upto the Third Five Year Plan, the NER does not figure explicitly in the development policy discourse. In the Fourth plan, the issue of balanced regional development comes to the centre stage. The focus was on how to secure the fullest possible utilization of the resources of each region so that it can contribute its best to the national pool and take its due share from the benefits accruing from national development. The reason behind backwardness of regions including the NER by implication was the failure to secure proper utilization of resources.

The Fifth Five Year Plan was a watershed for development in the North East. The NEC became operational. It was under the Home Ministry reflecting the obsessive concern for security among the policy makers. The concept of *sub plan* was introduced. Central assistance to the mountain areas was made more systematic. Even though the need for central assistance for development of mountain areas forming part of larger composite State as in Assam was recognized as early as the Second Five Year Plan, yet it was not systematized. It was recognized that the investments needed for meeting the infrastructural gaps in communications, transport, power generation and transmission, for the development of stable and diversified agriculture in place of jhum cultivation, horticulture, plantation crops and large scale afforestation was immense and there was no way these States can generate matching resources. This justifies the current practice of *central plan assistance* for the Special Category States. (Govt. of India, Sixth Five Year Plan, p.413)

During the Fifth and Sixth Five Year Plans, the economic policy of the region was part of the Hill area development programme which highlighted the issues of difficult terrain, agro-climatic conditions and historical lag in economic development and also the immense growth potential. Since the Seventh Five Year Plan it came under the Hill area development programme component of Special Area Development Programmes. The programmes during the Fifth Plan were beneficiary oriented. The emphasis shifted to eco-development in the Sixth Plan. The Seventh Plan emphasised the development of ecology and environment aiming at evolving programmes to take care of socio-economic growth, development of infrastructure and promotion of ecology of the region. This plan identified the basic tasks of the region as follows (i) attainment of self sufficiency in food; (ii) viable solution to the problem of shifting cultivation; (iii) ecological and environmental protection; (iv)reduction in infrastructural bottlenecks; (v) development of suitable small, village and cottage industries and generation of productive employment; and (vi) manpower development. During the Eighth Plan the focus was on productive sectors of the mountain economies by modernizing the agricultural practices and small scale industries at household, cottage and village levels.

The thrust areas during the Ninth Plan were: (i) eco-restoration and eco-preservation; (ii) involvement of the local population; (iii) gender sensitive planning; (iv) use of appropriate technology; (v) redevelopment of traditional agro-eco systems based on traditional knowledge and technology; (vi) scientific approach to agriculture, animal husbandry and horticulture in order to raise productivity; and (vii) development of ecologically sustainable industries and tourism. Since the mid-1990s the NER economic development began to find a place in the mainstream collective psyche. In October 1996 H.D. Deve Gowda, the then Prime Minister, announced an economic package of 6,100 crore for specific projects in the NER, and introduced North East sub plan in all central ministries for which 10% of their budgets would be earmarked for the region. In January 2000, Atal Behari Bajpayee further announced a Rs.10,271 crore package for the region. During the Tenth Plan, NER appeared as a category in special area programme. The focus shifted to improving implementation and ensuring better delivery of results, providing upstream assistance and policy support and strengthening capacity and public involvement. The Department of Development of the North Eastern Region (DONER) was set up in September 2001 to cater to the specific developmental needs of the NER. The North Eastern Council Act 1971 was amended in December 2002 to incorporate Sikkim as the eighth member. Since 2005 NEC has started functioning as a regional planning body. The preparation of State Development Reports and Human Development Reports for each of the states has given the opportunity for critically examining the State economies in a holistic manner than ever before.[22]

The "Peace, Progress and Prosperity in the Northeastern Region: Vision 2020," released by the Prime Minister in New Delhi on 2 July 2008 is a document which announces the outline of developmental policies aimed at reducing the developmental gap and reducing the infrastructural and connectivity deficit in Northeast India by the year 2020. The report identifies, as its focus areas, three broad categories of infrastructure, namely, transport and communication,

[22] Manipur and Mizoram are yet to produce the reports.

industry-related infrastructure, and infrastructure related to the provision of public amenities, all initiating and sustaining the growth process. The report acknowledges the fact that lack of communication is a major hindrance in the development of the region, thereby laying special focus on connectivity issues and related infrastructure. The construction of roads and railway lines, with a view to connect the State capitals in the region, has been given utmost priority in the report. The report recommends the creation of centres of excellence (educational institutions) in the region for developing their human resource which would help integrate the region better within current globalized processes and contexts. It highlights issues pertaining to capacity-building, people's participation in governance, creation of economic opportunities, and utilization of resources for the benefit of the local population of Northeast India.

The NER vision document puts forward a strategy comprising of five interdependent components for inclusive development of the region. They are:

(i) Participatory development articulated through grass-roots planning in which focus should be to develop the sectors and sub-sectors with comparative advantage;

(ii) Augmenting the capacity of the people to participate productively in the economic activities and creation and development of the institutions to design and implement developmental programmes as desired by the people;

(iii) Augmenting infrastructure, particularly connectivity and transport infrastructure to facilitate two-way movement of people and goods within the region and outside and open up markets for the produce in the region, attract private investments and create greater employment opportunities and choice for the people of the region;

(iv) Ensuring adequate flow of resources for public investments in infrastructure, implementing a framework for private participation in augmenting infrastructure and creating an enabling environment for the flow of investments to harness the physical resources of the region for the welfare of the people; and

(v) Transforming the governance by providing a secure, responsive and market friendly environment including protecting the property rights of the investors and ensuring a corruption free administration. Protecting the rights of the tribal for the use of land and forest resources is part·cularly important to ensure a sense of belonging and security to them.

For nearly two decades now, the Government of India, starting from Prime Minister P.V. Narasimha Rao in1992, have been talking of a Look East Policy with the objective of establishing closer economic integration with the South East Asian countries to begin with and now the East Asian countries as well but without exactly specifying the components and strategies of the policy. Since then LEP has gradually emerged as a policy alternative for unleashing the growth potential of the region through connectivity with the fast growing South East and East Asian markets.

NER enjoys special advantages over other parts of India in trade in view of India's Look East Policy (LEP) in general and India's economic engagement with her eastern neighbours through India-ASEAN Free Trade Agreement (FTA) and other bilateral FTAs in particular. NER's locational advantage and rich natural resources justify its development as a base for cooperation not only with the ASEAN but also with neighbouring countries such as Bangladesh, Bhutan, and Nepal. Regional cooperation cantering NER can be extended through Myanmar to Mekong region, comprising Cambodia, Lao PDR, Thailand, and Vietnam. NER can emerge as a strategic base for foreign as well as domestic investors to tap the world's largest market in South, South East and East Asia.

It may be argued that greater openness of an economy is potentially beneficial to all but we must realise that reaping the benefits requires appropriate policy designs followed by effective implementation. Evolution of a science and technology education policy and trade and infrastructure development in NER may be seen in this perspective. The cultural and demographic affinity, the geographic closeness and the potential advantages from intensified economic interactions can serve as catalysts for development of the region.

Over the past several years, a number of regional and sub-regional initiatives have been taken by countries in South and South East Asia, which would help shape the economic geography of the region. These include the enhanced cooperation among the members of the South Asian Association of Regional Cooperation (SAARC) that have agreed to set up a South Asian Economic Union, the Bay of Bengal Initiative for Multi-sectoral Technical and Economic Cooperation (BIMSTEC),[23] the Asia-Pacific Trade Agreement (APTA).[24] Providing fillip to these initiatives would necessitate NER playing a pivotal role (Figure 1.1), particularly so given the locational empirics of the region.

---

[23] Members of BIMSTEC are Bangladesh, India, Myanmar, Sri Lanka, Thailand, Bhutan and Nepal.

[24] Members are Bangladesh, India, Lao People's Democratic Republic, the Republic of Korea and Sri Lanka.

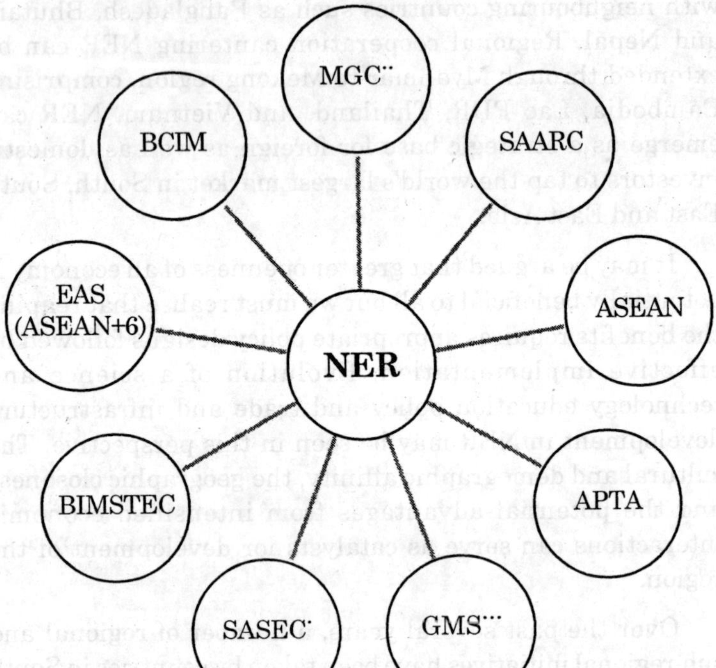

Fig.1: NER as India's Gateway to the East

Notes: * South Asia Sub-regional Economic Cooperation (SASEC)
** Mekong-Ganga Cooperation
***Greater Mekong Sub-region (GMS)

A rich body of literature argues that "trade-induced investment-led growth" was at the heart of the process of European integration project. More recently, India has also experienced deepening of its economic relations with Sri Lanka through "trade-induced investments". The India-Lanka Free Trade Agreement prompted Indian firms to establish their presence in Sri Lanka. Most notably, Indian Oil Corporation and several vegetable oil producers made sizeable investments. More recently, Sri Lankan investments have started flowing into India, which includes Brandix Sri Lanka, the largest textile exporter from the country. Trade induced investment in the NER and across the international borders may be equally relevant.

Conclusion

In spite of the shift in policy focus by New Delhi, however, the changes have not been able to bring about any significant change in the development deficit in Northeast India in the past few years. Why has this been the case? NER can escape from its present condition of underdevelopment and insurgency, only when several underlying problems are solved first. While the overarching policy framework has been expanded to include visions for Northeast India, it is necessary also to strengthen the political will of the concerned central government ministries and State governments to initiate and implement the policy recommendations. Critical to the success of the mission, would be concrete policies to back up the funds allocated, accompanied with much-needed coordination and unity among the State governments of Northeast India. There is an urgent need to make the economic policies work so that the process of alienation is reversed.

2

Demographic Picture of North East

—M. Hemanta Meitei & N. Deva Singh

Introduction

Demography is derived from the Greek word *demos* meaning people and hence is the science of population. Population study/demography discusses the changes in size of population and how the changes in the population are brought about? What is the significance of these changes from the points of human welfare? Where are people found? What are the changes taking place in their distribution in communities and in areas? What kind of people are found in any given population group and how do these in one group differ from those in the other.[25]

Main focused areas of demography are:

1. Size and forces related to the changes in size, its rate of change;

---

[25] Thomson, Warren S. (1953), *Population Problems,* McGraw Mountains Co., New York.

2. Distribution of population – why and how the distribution arise as a result of both different rates of natural growth and also through migration, both internally within countries and at the international scale;
3. Composition and characteristics of population – its internal structures of age and sex, of how youthful and ageing population structures emerge, and how and why these have different development implications; and
4. The ability of population as a result of their skills and knowledge base and culture to contribute to own economic and social well-being.

These areas clearly indicate that the study of population is concerned with its size or numbers, its structure and characteristics, its distribution and the changes taking place in it over a period of time. It is also implied in these description that the subject matter of population studies includes the study of fertility, mortality, migration and social mobility. One important area of study covers the component of population change or the factors responsible for change in the size of population. It must be understood that the population of any place at a specific time is a function of three types of events -- births, deaths and migration. There are four ways in which the number of people in any area can undergo change: (1) children may be born in that area, (2) the inhabitants of that area may die, (3) people from other areas may move into that area, and (4) people of that area may move out of that area. It is equally important to understand the concept of population structure and characteristics. Population structure implies the age and sex structure of the population, marital status, literacy and educational status, labour force status, etc.

Relationship between Development and Population

The relationships between population and development are of cause and effect in both directions: development can affect population and population can affect development. These relationships are reflexive and there is a flow of causality from population to development and also from development to population. Population will affect development in various ways: its size and its rate of growth, its distribution, its age and sex structure, its capability to work and contribute to the economic and social changes that are part and parcel of development. These characteristics of the population of an area will inevitably affect the nature, style and pace of actual and any potential development.

It must be immediately recognised that population is only one of a range of possible variables that affect and are affected by development. Population must be considered along with the volume, values and range of financial and environmental resources, the quality of governance and other major development factors in the development effort. Population does always have some effect on development. Its effect can be variable in its intensity or direction; it can be large, it can be slight, or even neutral; it can be positive, a beneficial factor, or it can be negative, a constraint on development.

There is also a relationship that development will also affect population. Mortality will be reduced by better living standards, better food security and environmental conditions and by better medical practice and health care provision. Fertility will also be affected directly by quality of health care, especially in provision of contraceptive and reproductive health services, and indirectly, but much more fundamentally, by changing patterns of economy and society. Migration will be affected by changing conditions at the source and destination of the migrants. Some locations become less attractive as places to live and work while others, mostly towns in the case of internal migration and richer countries where jobs are available in the case of international migration, become more attractive. That development is a key driver of natural population change (fertility and mortality) is one of the basic assumptions of demographic transition theory[26] and it shows the relationship between the births and deaths (growth of population).

Development Studies and Population Studies

In order to provide a better baseline for understanding the reflexive nature of population and development relationships it will be helpful to situate these issues in the context of the two academic disciplines of Development Studies and Population Studies, and the interface between them. Neither Development Studies nor Population Studies have traditionally been seen as mainstream academic disciplines. They are rather taken as branches of larger disciplines, of economics in the case of Development Studies, and of sociology, geography or statistical demography in the case of Population Studies. However, over the years Development Studies and Population Studies have their own professional associations, nationally and globally, and also have their own core of methods and materials, including major journals in their fields. These are all the hallmarks of growth and cohesion of independent disciplines, but in both these cases there is a stronger sense now than there has ever been in the traditional disciplines of looking outwards towards a more multidisciplinary perspective.

The Growth of Population Studies

Population Studies as a body of knowledge and cohesive theory has also experienced changes in content, context and

---

[26] It is a theory specifying that societies progress from a pre-modern regime of high fertility and high mortality to a post-modern regime of low fertility and low mortality.

approach, but over a longer period than Development Studies. The beginnings of Population Studies, though not conceptualised as such at the time, were set in the late eighteenth century with the intellectual controversies over the causes and impacts of the French Revolution of 1789. T.R. Malthus himself developed his ideas about the nature of poverty as a response to the socialist writings of William Godwin, who argued that unequal distribution of power in society was the root cause of poverty. Malthus in reply argued that the poor were largely responsible for their own poverty, and that population growth would in the long run generate even greater poverty and inequality as the population would outstrip the resources on which they could survive. This recurring debate was integrated into mainstream economic thought in the nineteenth century, but the Malthusian threat of overpopulation receded substantially in that period as new land in the New World and the technology of supplies of food to the rapidly growing populations of Europe. Development seemed to be positively associated with population growth.

Terminologies commonly used in Demography

Fertility: The actual reproductive performance of an individual, a couple, a group, or a population.

Crude Birth Rate: The number of live births per 1,000 population in a given year.

Crude Death Rate: The number of deaths per 1,000 population in a given year.

Natural Increase: The surplus (or deficit) of births over deaths in a population in a given time period.

Population Increase: The total population increase resulting from the interaction of births, deaths, and migration in a population in a given period of time.

Rate of Natural Increase (or Decrease): The rate at which a population is increasing (or decreasing) in a given year due to a surplus (or deficit) of births over deaths, expressed as a percentage of the base population.

Carrying capacity: The maximum sustainable size of a resident population in a given ecosystem.

Infant Mortality Rate: The number of deaths of infants under age 1 per 1,000 live births in a given year.

Life expectancy: The average number of additional years a person could expect to live if current mortality trends were to continue for the rest of that person's life. Most commonly cited as life expectancy at birth.

Migration: The movement of people across a specified boundary for the purpose of establishing a new or semi-permanent residence. It is divided into international migration (migration between countries) and internal migration (migration within a country).

Mobility: The geographic movement of people.

Population Explosion: Expressions used to describe the 20th century worldwide trend of rapid population growth, resulting from a world birth rate much higher than the world death rate.

Population Momentum: The tendency for population growth to continue beyond the time that replacement-level fertility has been achieved because of the relatively high concentration of people in the childbearing years.

Total Fertility Rate: The average number of children that would be born alive to a woman (or group of women) during her lifetime if she were to pass through her childbearing years conforming to the age-specific fertility rates of a given year.

Urban: Countries differ in the way they classify population as "urban" or "rural." Typically, a community or settlement with a population of 2,000 or more is considered urban. A listing of country definitions is published annually in the United Nations Demographic Yearbook. In India census definition of urban areas (a) all places with a Municipality, Corporation or Cantonment or Notified Town Area (b) all other places which satisfied the following criteria- (i) a minimum population of 5,000, (ii) at least 75 % of the male working population was working in non-agricultural activity and (iii) a density of population of at least 400 sq. km. (i.e. 1000 per sq. mile).

Urbanisation: Growth in the proportion of a population living in urban areas and the process involved.

Sources for the Study of Population and Development

There is no shortage of basic data and useful discussion of population and development taken separately and of population and development relationships taken together. Much of the baseline data and illustrative material can be found on public access in the web pages of the major international organisations: the World Bank, in its Health and Population Division; the UN in its Population Division; and also in the data provided by the UN Development Programme (UNDP) and the UN Population Fund (UNFPA). In the US, the US Bureau of the Census (International Division) and the Population Reference Bureau are important and easily accessible sources of data and analysis. Another major US site is associated with the international programme of Demographic and Health Surveys (DHS) at its website: www.measuredhs.com. Here there is access to national reports from around the world and summary technical documents.

People of North-East India

Population of NER States has multiethnic and multilingual characteristics and is more or less a miniature replica of the Indian sub-continent. Right from the early times, in spite of its secluded geographical location, people from dissimilar ethnic stocks with diverse socio-cultural backgrounds came from different directions at various stages and established their colonization. The region served as a corridor where migrants from Tibet, South East Asia and China and Indian sub-continent arrived at and made their permanent abode. The varied topographical features of the region are responsible to have various socio-cultural backgrounds of different ethnics.

It is believed that the Mon Khmer group of Austro Asiatic linguistic groups are believed to be the earliest settlers of North-east India. The Khasis and Jaintias of Meghalaya of today are of this group. Next arrivals were the Mongoloids from the North-and east, who belong to the Tibeto-Burman language-speaking people. They settled over the mountain and plain areas and belonged to Adis, Mishims, Apatanis etc. of Arunachal Pradesh, Chutiyas, Boro Kacharies, Dimasas, Bodo etc. of Assam, Nagas of Nagaland, Meities and Kukichin speakers including Mizo, Hmar etc. of Manipur and Mizoram. Waves of migration of Tai-Ahom people of Sino-Siamese branch from the Shan plateau and Kukichin groups from upper Burma continued upto the 18th century in the region.[27] The Caucasoid or the Indo-Aryans started gradually entering from the west i.e., the Indian mainland, with higher intensity in the beginning of the 13th century, who have brought Hindu culture and mingled with the early settlers. These three broad groups of people arrived at the northeast region make the composite pattern of cultural synthesis and evolution.

During historical periods, Burmese invasions and fighting among the kingdoms or dominant groups had destroyed the

---

[27] Bhattacharyya, N.N. (2005): *North East India: A Systematic Geography*, Rajesh Publications, New Delhi.

economy and disseminated the population that eventually led to out-migrate the earlier settlers outside the kingdom e.g., Manipur met seven years devastation in the hand of Burmese from 1819 to 1825 A.D.

Peopling of the region is very much concerned with the streams and waves of immigration that took place during historical periods and subsequent distribution of population in the region. The existing physiographic has maintained the inter-group differences having agglomerated on some localities by particular groups and disperses population on some other localities and areas. The British India landed on this part of world in 1826, since then movement of people from India, Bangladesh and Nepal virtually began for the construction of motor able roads, railway lines, and opening of Tea gardens in Assam, which were largely to fulfil the requirements of British personal and the colonial administrative, commercial and political objectives in the North-east India. Thus, thousands of Assam Tea garden's labourers from Chhotanagpur plateau, who belong mostly to the Mundari language - speaking group of the Austro-Asiatic ethnolinguistics family around 1850.s, migration of landless peasants from the then East Bengal, now Bangladesh in 1870's to occupy islands and flood plains from Dhubri district to Lakhimpur district, Assam and the immigration of thousands of Hindu refugees from East Pakistan following the partition of the country in 1947 have disturbed in the distribution of population and socio-cultural lives of the inhabitants. A few remarkable changes in the population and settlement structure were also witnessed during the post-independence period. The instances are fleeing of large scale Bangali Hindus to Assam and other states of Northeast India due to discrimination against the religious minorities and the war of liberation of Bangladesh.

The complex physiographic conditions of the eastern Himalayan ranges of Sikkim, Arunachal Pradesh, etc., the

Indo-Myanmar mountains of Nagaland, Manipur, Mizoram and Tripura, the plateau of Meghalaya and the Brahmaputra valley have provided ideal environment for the settlements of a large number of communities. They have habitats in mountains in varying degrees of isolation and primitive modes of economy and river valleys and plains of easily accessible areas where assimilation of successive waves have left the imprint of complex pattern of population composition with comparatively advance economic situation supported by agriculture and good transport and communication system.

So the region has exhibited accumulation of a number of groups of people and at present a minimum of 357 constitutional communities including 32 scheduled castes and 182 scheduled tribes are in the region (excluding Sikkim). They are the Tibeto-Burman groups of Arunachal Pradesh, Nagaland, Manipur, Mizoram, Sikkim, parts of Meghalaya and Assam, the Indo-Aryan groups in the valley areas of the Brahmaputra, Cachar and Tripura plains and the Mon Khmer group, south of the Brahmaputra valley in Khasia and Jaintia mountains.[28]

Population Growth and Distribution

In terms of the absolute number the population of the NER has been growing over time. As shown in Table-2.1 all the states have been experiencing the growth of population in terms of the absolute number. About four per cent (3.76%) of total population of the country is contributed from this region compared to the 8% of geographical area. Ever since 1951 census, the highest number of population has been contributed by Assam and followed by Tripura. In other words, the distribution of population in this region is sparse. According to the 2011 the population of Assam is 31 millions compared

[28] Goel, N.P and Gopalakrishnan, R. (2003): *Geography of North East India*, Ansu Publications, Smountainong.

Table 2.1
Population of North East India from 1901 to 2011
(in thousand)

Year	*Arunachal Pradesh*	*Assam*	*Manipur*	*Meghalaya*	*Mizoram*	*Nagaland*	*Sikkim*	*Tripura*	*NE Total*	*India*
1901	—	3290	284	341	82	102	59	173	4331	238396
1911	—	3849	346	394	91	149	88	230	5147	252093
1921	—	4637	384	422	98	159	82	304	6086	251321
1931	—	5560	446	481	124	179	110	382	7282	278977
1941	—	6695	512	556	153	190	122	513	8741	318661
1951	—	8029	578	606	196	213	138	639	10399	361088
1961	337	10837	780	769	266	369	162	1142	14662	439235
1971	468	14625	1073	1012	332	516	210	1556	19792	548160
1981	632	18041	1421	1336	494	775	316	2053	23788	683329
1991	865	22414	1837	1775	690	1210	406	2757	31954	846303
2001	1098	26656	2294	2319	889	1990	541	3199	38986	1028737
2011	1383	31169	2722	2964	1091	1981	608	3671	45588	1210193

Source: Registrar General of India

to only 3.67 millions in Tripura, 2.96 in Meghalaya and 2.72 millions in Manipur. The least is in Sikkim with less than one million population (6.1 lakh). The increase in population over time is due to the excess births over deaths along with immigration of population other states of the country or other countries.

The growth of population in the region is higher than the national average (Table 2.2). Recent population data from the 2011 census clearly establish this. High population growth is a national concern in terms of sustainable development. When the population largely has witnessed the decline in the general death rate, the birth rate will overshadow the death rate. This creates a huge margin of natural growth rate leading to a large net addition of population. The greatest challenge being faced along with the population growth is the rapid expansion in the younger age group specially the child population and resulting large volume of population in reproductive age group who have the potential for further increase of population. Here is the need for controlling the rapid pace of birth rate for the decline in population size in the absence of net addition due to migration.

The annual exponential growth rate ever since 1971-81 census shows, except for Assam, that the growth rate of population in all the States is higher than the national average. The Table-2.2 also shows that over the time there has been a decline in the growth rate of population in all these States. Among the notable States perhaps Nagaland shows an unpredictable declinc of population in 2011 census. There is no exact reason behind this. However, it is quite clear that a State which has a recorded growth rate of above 4% ever since 1971 census will see a sudden decline to a negative growth is very much doubtful. Available data on natural increase coupled with infant mortality rate donot support it. However, it may be concluded that Nagaland might have experienced a mass exodus of population in the

Table 2.2
Growth Rate of Population in the North Eastern Region

State	Decadal growth rate				Annual exponential growth rate			
	1971-81	*1981-91*	*1991-2001*	*2001-11*	*1971-81*	*1981-91*	*1991-2001*	*2001-11*
Arunachal Pradesh	35.15	36.83	27.00	25.92	3.01	3.14	2.39	2.33
Assam	23.36	24.24	18.92	16.93	2.10	2.17	1.73	1.58
Manipur	32.46	29.29	24.86	18.65	2.81	2.57	2.22	1.72
Meghalaya	32.04	32.86	30.65	27.82	2.78	2.84	2.67	2.49
Mizoram	48.55	39.70	28.82	22.78	3.96	3.34	2.53	2.07
Nagaland	50.05	56.08	64.53	-0.47	4.06	4.45	4.98	-0.05
Sikkim	31.92	34.30	16.03	12.36	2.77	2.95	1.49	1.17
Tripura	50.77	24.47	33.06	14.75	4.11	2.51	2.86	1.39
India	24.66	23.85	21.54	17.64	2.2	2.14	1.93	1.64

Source: Registrar General of India

intercensal interval for internal or external migration. This is a classic case of understanding the demographic phenomenon of the population of a particular geographical area.

Except for Nagaland which records negative growth rate during the last intercensal period between 2001 and 2011 other States like Mizoram, Meghalaya, and Arunachal Pradesh exhibit higher growth rate above 2%. The rest of the States such as Sikkim, Tripura, Assam and Manipur record a growth rate less than 2%. This clearly shows that in the absence of the massive migration to these States the growth rate of population will be experiencing a declining growth rate in these States in future.

Another feature of the population growth rate on the basis of the exponential growth is the implication of time to double the population size. Roughly it can be calculated as 70 divided by the growth rate. As an example the national level growth rate is 1.64 and using this growth rate and putting it into the formula we get 70/1.64 equal to 44.4 years. This implies that if the India continues to grow its population at the same rate it will take about 41.4 years to double the size of population. This means that there will 2.42 billion population by 2052. Keeping this clue Sikkim will have twice the current size of population after 60 years whereas Meghalaya will take only 28 years to double its population given the current rate of growth.

Population distribution in the NER is largely a reflection of the history of settlement of the people and their activities in various economic development programmes. With the increase of population, density of people living per square kilometre area also increases gradually in all the eight States as seen table 2.3. Of the total area, 262,179 sq. km. constituting nearly 28 per cent mainly plain areas accommodate about 32 million population and the mountains and mountains, about 72 per cent area support 13 million people who are mostly of scheduled tribes. The tribal population varies from 25 per cent in the plain areas to above 80 per cent in mountainous States like Mizoram, Arunachal Pradesh and Nagaland. The region has an average density of 174 persons per sq. km. in 2011 (Table-2.3).

Table 2.3
North-East India: Density of Population, 1981-2011 (per km²)

State / Country	*2011*	*2001*	*1991*	*1981*
Arunachal Pradesh	17	13	10	8
Assam	397	340	286	230
Manipur	122	103	82	64
Meghalaya	132	103	79	60
Mizoram	52	43	33	23
Nagaland	119	120	73	47
Sikkim	86	76	57	45
Tripura	350	305	263	196
NER	174	151		
India	382	325	267	216

Sources: i) Census of India, 2001 and 2011, Primary Census Abstract, Total Population, Table A-5 and ii) Census of India, 2011: Provisional Population Totals, Series-I.

Barring the general poverty and ethnic diversity, Assam has been recording high density of population above the national average in the last four decades. The most sparsely populated among the States and Union Territories in the country is Arunachal Pradesh being found 17 persons per sq. km. in 2011. Unevenness of concentration of population is the typical feature of the region. The fertile plain of the Brahmaputra valley represents the central heartland of the region, along with Cachar plain, Tripura plain and Manipur valley. The chief governing factors are availability of cultivable land with fertile soils, well accessibility to provisions for goods and services to the inhabitants, and good transport network to develop urban centres. The outlying mountains and upland mountain topography generally face difficulty in getting cultivable land, roads over the zigzag terrain, and face isolation and forest cover. In spite of such deterrents, various small urban portions are developing into mountain stations, and pocket mountain valleys are emerging as acute population concentration with the improvement of socio-economic conditions among the mountain States. As such degree of high variability in the density of population exists in the region.

In 2011, Assam has the largest population, 31.16 million due to its location and vast plain areas and is recorded 397 persons per sq. km. followed by Tripura (350), Manipur (120) and Meghalaya (132) both in population and density. The smallest State, Sikkim, has 0.60 million population with the density of 86 person per sq. km. Arunachal Pradesh is the biggest State in the region with the lowest density (17 persons per sq. km.) mainly due to rugged mountainous areas where distribution of human settlements is very sparse.

Population distribution is in response to the age-old pattern of habitation and utilization of local resources for a variety of purposes, for which homogenous plain areas and a good transport network are required. A good example is the Manipur valley where the four districts, Imphal West, Thoubal, Imphal East and Bishnupur got population and density 847, 713, 555 and 415 persons respectively per sq. km. in 2001. Because of influx of migrants from the south to the fertile plains along the Brahmaputra valley in Assam, density abovc 500 persons per sq. km. is found in districts of Nagaon, Dhubri, Kamrup, Barpeta and Nalbari. Similarly in Cachar plain, Karimganj district and West Tripura in Tripura population density were above the State averages. Many of the plain districts, where agriculture is advanced more than the adjoining areas and where urban centres are developed with better connectivity of roads and railway connections, are found high density above 300 persons per sq. km. These districts include Goalpara, Bongaigaon, Darrang, Marigaon, Sonitpur, Jorhat, Cachar, Hailakandi in Assam and even Dimapur in Nagaland. In Assam, except Karbi Anglong and North-Cachar Mountains district, all have density more than 175 persons per sq. km. The entire Arunachal Pradesh is mountain area, so the density was below 50 persons per sq. km. and at Dibang Valley and Siang districts, the densities were 4 and 5 persons, lowest in the region. The similar distribution pattern of population was found in many mountain districts of Nagaland, Mizoram, Meghalaya and Manipur with a little higher density of population. Whenever, there are townships with good road connectivity, the density may be higher, e.g., East Khasi mountains and West Garo mountains districts of Meghalaya and Aizawal district in Mizoram. The Tripura plain as a whole was comparatively high in density of population having found above 130 persons per sq. km. in all the four districts in 2001.

There were 40,262 villages and 254 towns distributed all over the areas of Northeast India; as many as 32,771,156 rural population and 6,086,613 urban population live in these settlements in 2001. Occupying 98.74% of rural areas, 84.33% of the total population live in mountains and plains of the region and in each of the seven constituent states the rural population is high. Nearly 15 per cent of the total population of the region concentrate in about 0.5 per cent of urban area. All the capital cities with above one lakh population are connected well by roads. Numerous mountain villages do not have large population sizes. For instance, 90 per cent of rural population of Arunachal Pradesh and Meghalaya concentrate in villages less than 2000 population. However, all the states of North-east region have population distribution more than 60 per cent between the size class of villages, 500 and 5,000 population. The population distribution among the villages above the size of 5,000 which have the potential to emerge to urban status is comparatively more in Tripura, Manipur, Nagaland and Assam than other States in 2001.

Thus, the population in the region is unevenly distributed. There is high degree of population concentration in the central portion, river basins and pocket plains where economic conditions are better than the peripheral, interior mountain and mountainous territories. Sparse distribution of population of negligible concentration is found due to difficulties of mountainous terrain with isolation and inaccessibility.

The question ahead is not the growth rate as such but the relative significance of the population growth. Both the policy makers and general public have to seek the solutions for such issues as these States cannot afford increase of population at this rate? Are we prepared for the growth rate leading to rapid growth? Will there be enough resources to feed this population, are there enough infrastructural facilities to ensure a quality life — basic education, health facility, social security, a steady growth of per capita income to the level of the developed countries?

Age and Sex Distribution

Sex ratio (number of males per female) is one of the important parameters of the population composition in terms of gender. It shows parity in size of population between male and female populations. With a fairly constant sex ratio at birth of about 105 and a sex ratio of deaths in the range 105 to 125, the sex ratio of a population will fall near 100 in the absence of migration. Biologically there is parity between the sexes in the long run. But at birth the sex ratio is in favour of males to the females. However in due course of life the incidence of dying between the sexes differs and females outlive the males. Therefore, at the end the sex ratio is in favour of the females particularly in the older ages. In the context of the sex ratio analysis it is pertinent to answer the question that how much of the advantage of males at birth will have a lasting impact on sex ratio of the population.

In the Indian context the sex ratio is termed as number of females to the number of males while in the international convention it is number of males to the number of females. The trend in last two censuses of the NER shows that there is an increase in the sex ratio. But this should not be taken as a different case since the overall sex ratio of India has improved in the last two censuses. The increase in the sex ratio is quite substantial in the States of Arunachal Pradesh and Mizoram while other States have shown a similar level of increase in the sex ratio (Table-2.4). Of late there is an improvement, though marginal, in the overall life expectancy of females in India over the males. The improvement in sex ratio of the population is not sufficient to cherish since there is a major blow in the sex ratio of the child population of less than 7 years. In this bracket over last one decade of intercensal period there is a substantial decline in the sex ratio of 0-6 old population from 927 to 914. If the international standard of sex ratio at birth of 105 males per 100 female babies is maintained then at birth the sex ratio might have been recorded about 952 females per 1,000 male babies born. Again the under 5 mortality in the country is higher among the females than the males with a margin of about 10 points. However, this pattern of experience is not observed in case of NER States except for Assam. According to the NFHS-3, in all these the mortality of boys is higher than the girls of the same age. Given the international sex ratio at birth benchmark, for the States where child sex ratio is higher than 952 (F/M) is not a major concern. This should be linked with age reporting recorded in the census which more often than not tends to misreporting. But in a setting, with less gender bias, of NER it is perceived that there should not be substantial difference in age misreporting according to the sex of the children.

Table 2.4
Sex Ratio of the Population in the NER, 2001 and 2011

	Sex Ratio		*0-6 Population*		*7+ Population*	
State	*2001*	*2011*	*2001*	*2011*	*2001*	*2011*
Arunachal Pradesh	893	920	964	960	878	913
Assam	935	952	965	957	929	953
Manipur	978	987	957	934	977	995
Meghalaya	972	986	973	970	971	989
Mizoram	935	975	964	971	930	976
Nagaland	900	931	964	944	890	929
Sikkim	875	889	963	944	861	883
Tripura	948	961	966	953	945	962
India	933	940	927	914	934	944

Source: Registrar General of India

Age is arguably the most important variable in the study of mortality, fertility, and certain other areas of demographic analysis. Tabulations on age are essential in the computation of the basic measures relating to the factors of population change, in the analysis of the factors of labour supply, and in the study of the problem of economic dependency. Many types of planning, such as military planning, planning of community institutions and services, particularly health services, and planning of sales programs require separate population data for males and females and for different age groups. Age is an important variable in measuring potential school population, the potential voting population and potential manpower. Age data are required for preparing current population estimates and projections; projections of households, school enrolment, and labour force, as well as projections of requirements for schools, teachers, health services, food, and housing.

Social scientists also have a special interest in the age and sex structure of a population, because social relationships within a community are considerably affected by the relative numbers of males and females and the relative numbers at each age. The sociologist and the economist have a vital

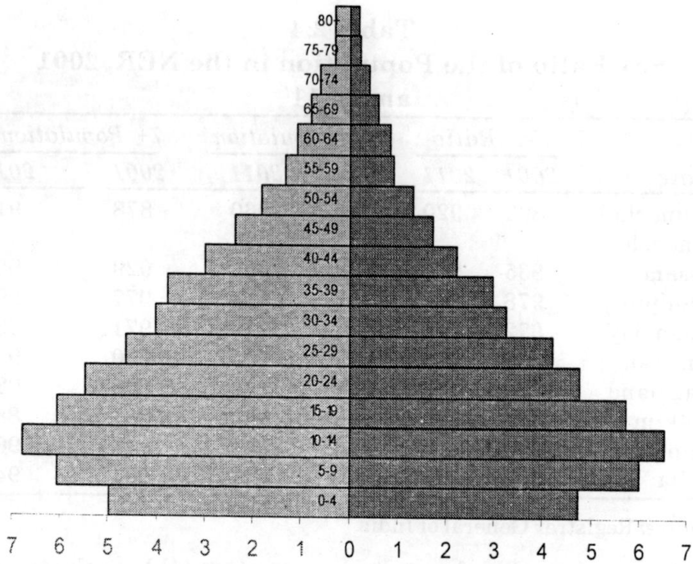

Fig. 1: Population pyramid of Sikkim, 2001

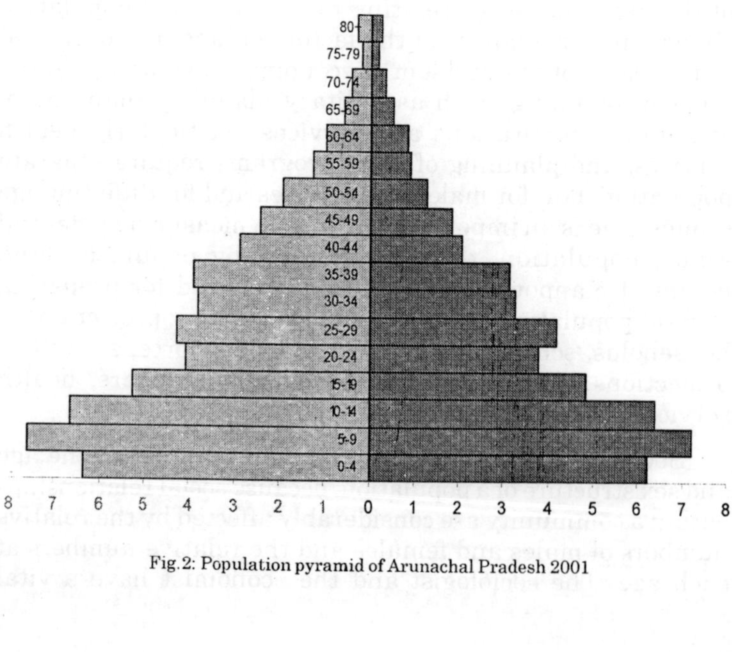

Fig. 2: Population pyramid of Arunachal Pradesh 2001

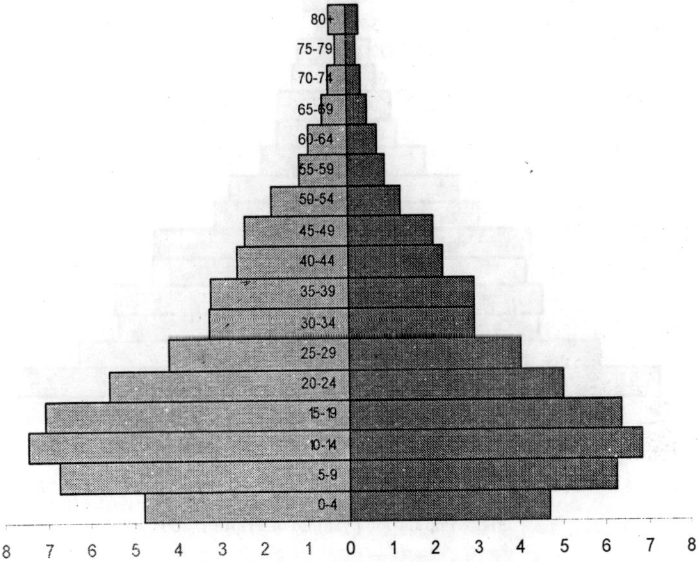

Fig.3: Population pyramid of Nagaland, 2001

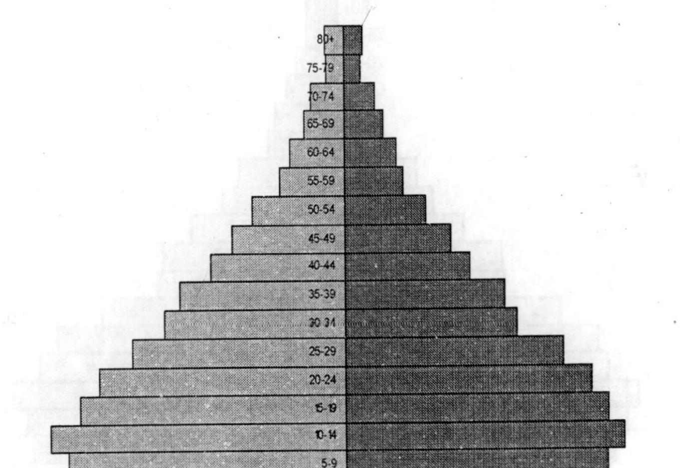

Fig.4: Population pyramid of Manipur, 2001

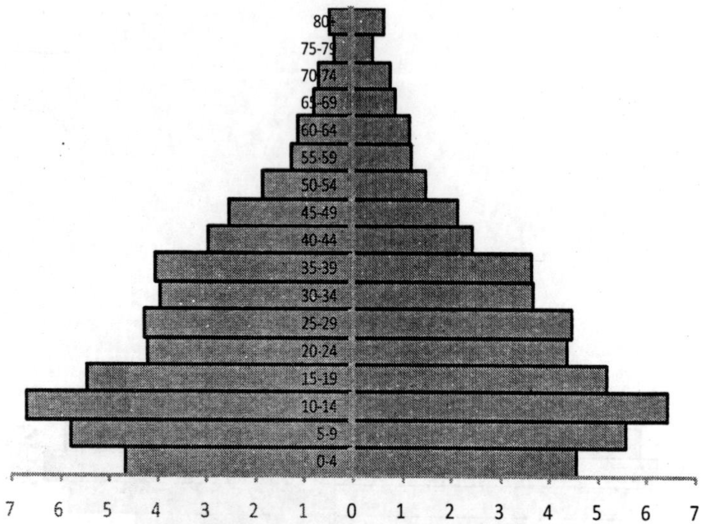

Fig.5: Population pyramid of Tripura, 2001

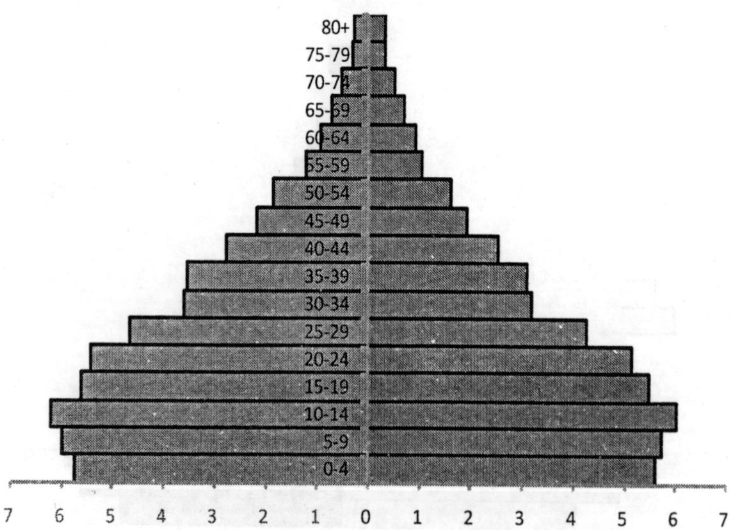

Fig.6: Population pyramid of Mizoram, 2001

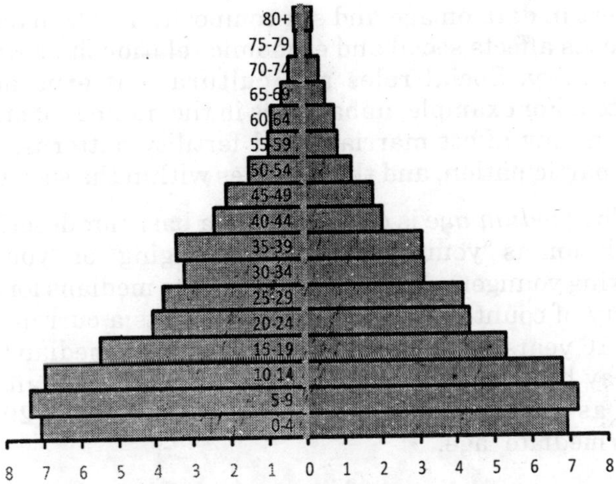

Fig.7: Population pyramid of Meghalaya, 2001

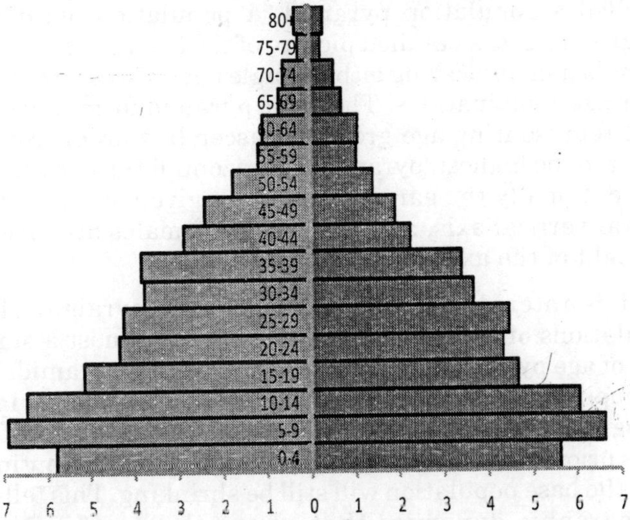

Fig.8: Population pyramid of Assam, 2001

Note: The left side of the pyramid represents male and right side represents female. The base shows the percentage to the total population.

interest in data on age and sex composition. The balance of the sexes affects social and economic relationships within a community. Social roles and cultural patterns may be affected. For example, imbalances in the number of men and women may affect marriage and fertility patterns, labour force participation, and the sex roles within the society.

The *median age* is often used as a basis for describing a population as "young" or "old" or as "aging" or "younging" (growing younger). An examination of the medians for a wide variety of countries around 1990 suggests a current range from 16 years to 38 years. Populations with medians under 20 may be described as "young," those with medians 30 or over as "old," and those with medians 20 to 29 as of "intermediate" age.

A very effective and quite widely used method of graphically depicting the age-sex composition of a population is called a population pyramid. A population pyramid is designed to give a detailed picture of the age-sex structure of a population, indicating either single ages, 5-year groups, or other age combinations. The basic pyramid form consists of bars, representing age groups in ascending order from the lowest to the highest, pyramided horizontally on one another. Conventionally the bars for males are given on the left of a central vertical axis, and the bars for females are given on the right of the axis.

It is interesting to observe the age pyramid of the populations of the States. They represent almost a similar kind of age pyramids. It is very clear from the pyramids that the population of the NER are experiencing a decline in the young age groups particularly of the recent births of five years prior to the 2001 census. If this age structure continues, then the base population will still be shrinking. This tells the demographic dynamics that, given the death rate and migration rate constant, the growth rate of population of the region will decline in the future. However, it is not known how far population will experience a declining trend of fertility resulting in reduction of growth rate. Given this trend it can be anticipated that the stabilisation of population will soon be a reality. The population will also experience a demographic bonus of a large size of working population while young dependency ratio is declining though old age dependency is rising.

Age distribution of a population serves as a basis for sound understanding of the economic characteristics of the population. Broadly any population may be classified on the basis of the number of economically active population and dependant population. The economically active population is often defined as those persons who are able to actively participate in any economic activity. This section of population usually lies between ages 15 and 60 or 65 years. Implicitly it implies that those who are not in the working age group are in the dependant group. They are no doubt important but they are heavily dependant on the working age population. Note that all the persons in the working age group are not in the labour force. In the population of NER the proportion of the young age (who are in less than 15 years old) constitutes a substantial section of the population. For example this proportion is highest in Assam (42.36%) followed by Arunachal Pradesh (40.37%). Other States have a relatively lower level of young age population but all of them have proportions above 30%. This means that about one-third of the population in these States are in the young age population.[29] One thing for sure is that the high concentration of population in this age demands a heavy investment on human capital formation in the short and long run, and provided this is fulfilled, then the population in today's young population will be a capable human capital of the future. Otherwise this should be a big problem in the future with a large number of unemployment and unrest in the social system and high rate of reproduction.

The above discussion of the high concentration of the young population is evident from the point of the dependency ratio of the young population to the working age population

[29] Whether this will be treated as a problem or a blessing depends on the way how the development strategists feel in these States and the policy-makers frame policies.

of age 15-59. This is relative very high in States like Meghalaya (79.81%), Arunachal Pradesh (73.3%) and Assam (66.1%), while in the rest of the region it is above 50%. This shows that the relative income of the people who are feeding will have to bear a major burden for supporting the young age population. This is not all. There is also a group of persons in the ageing category who normally retire from the economically active life. Such persons are known as old age population. They associate with old age dependency ratio. This is the ratio of population in age 60 and above to the working population. In India abouț 7% of the total population belong to the age group of 60 plus category according to the 2001 census. With the improvement in the life expectancy and standard of living their proportion also rises. In the NER also 5 out of 8 States about 5% of the population is from the 60 plus population (Table-2.5). Meanwhile the old age dependency has risen well above 8% in 7 States barring only Nagaland. The highest old age dependency is observed in Tripura (12.33%) followed by Manipur (11.1%) and Assam (10.34%). Therefore there is a need for a consideration of policy to address to the needs of this section. Old age population is often associated with a lot of wisdom and this must be tapped for a better productivity of the society.

Table 2.5

Distribution of Population by Age and Dependency Ratio according to 2001 Census

	Proportion of population in broad age groups			*Dependency ratio*	
	0-14	*15-59*	*60+*	*Young*	*Old*
Arunachal Pradesh	40.37	55.08	4.55	73.30	8.26
Assam	37.45	56.69	5.86	66.05	10.34
Manipur	32.68	60.59	6.73	53.94	11.10
Meghalaya	42.36	53.08	4.57	79.81	8.60
Mizoram	35.34	59.14	5.52	59.75	9.34
Nagaland	36.69	58.76	4.55	62.44	7.74
Sikkim	35.05	59.56	5.39	58.86	9.05
Tripura	33.67	59.05	7.30	57.02	12.33
India	35.44	57.09	7.47	62.09	13.08

Source: Calculated from the Census Age Tables

Literacy

Education is another vehicle to gear up the pace of development in the region. So far, the infrastructure available for it was not adequate, though there were missionary educational institutions in some selected places of the NER besides governments to open various general educational institutions, lower to higher levels and some technical institutions. In the last a few decades, many private institutions have come up competing with the missionaries in providing education. Moreover, each State of the North-east has opened Central University recently for higher education and research, and a few technical institutions for Medical and Engineering courses. Even then, the overall educational system and the support infrastructures are comparatively inferior to the rest of the world. Thus the rural poor and females in both mountains and plains are low in literacy. Based on the census data, 2001 and 2011, the standard of education in this part of the country can be examined. The Indian census follows the definition of literacy according to the functional literacy such that a person can be defined literate if he/she can read and write with understanding in any language. It defines the criterion by certain age and therefore since 1991 literacy will refer to the persons who have completed six years of age.

The region now has 9,516,084 illiterates of below aged 7 years and not attending any school. The trend of literacy level in the eight States of the region has been above the national average recording 70.73 per cent and 75.60 per cent in 2001 and 2011 respectively as compared to the respective national averages of 64.83 and 74.04 (Table-2.6). Of the 35 States and Union territories of the country, Mizoram stands in the third rank with 91.58 per cent and Tripura in the fourth rank. But the two States, Assam and Arunachal Pradesh, fall below 75 per cent of literacy in 2011, largely due to the uneducated rural population.

Gender gap in education is reflected well by the literacy percentages by sex. This is visible in the region as well. It is, however, interesting to note that both male and female illiterates in the region have decreased; in the case of male from 4,623627 to 3,833,551 and female from 6,746,734 to 5,682,533 reflecting the tendency that all States of the region are progressing in spite of different levels of literacy between the two. It is found that Mizoram, Nagaland and Meghalaya, the gender difference of literacy between male and female is less than 10 per centage points that proves that Christians majority States have lesser gender gap than the proportionately larger Hindu populated States. In the last decade Sikkim has got tremendous increase of female education from 15.64 per cent to 76.43 per cent. No State in the region has 15 percentage point gender gap in literacy except Arunachal Pradesh. Higher literacy is associated with low gender gap in education as depicted in Mizoram and Tripura. Assam and Arunachal Pradesh are still below 70 per cent of female education, the rest is above it in 2011 census. For narrowing down the gender gap in literacy to 10 percentage points and below by 2015 in the country according to the Millennium Development Goals of the United Nations, the Planning Commission of India has targeted to increase literacy rate of persons of age 7 years and above to 85 per cent by 2011-12. Since four States of North-east India have already crossed 85 per cent and four States are below the target, development in education in the region is another milestone for future hope of socio-economic growth and development.

Work Participation

The work participation rate of the country according to the 2001 census was only 39% though it was much higher among males. The gender difference in work participation rate is wide, and only one-fourth of women were working compared to the male participation. However, in all the States of the region, except for Assam and Tripura, the work participation of women was much higher than what was observed in the national level (Table 2.7). This shows the nature of gender equality arising out of active participation of women in economic activities in the region.

Table 2.6
North-East India, Literacy, 1991-2011

State	2011			2001			1991		
	Persons	*Male*	*Female*	*Persons*	*Male*	*Female*	*Persons*	*Male*	*Female*
Arunachal Pradesh	66.95	73.69	59.57	54.34	63.83	43.53	41.6	51.5	26.7
Assam	73.18	78.81	67.27	63.25	71.28	54.61	52.9	61.9	43.0
Manipur	79.85	86.49	73.17	69.93	79.54	60.10	59.9	71.6	47.6
Meghalaya	75.48	77,17	73.78	62.56	65.43	59.61	49.1	53.1	44.9
Mizoram	91.58	93.72	89.40	88.80	90.72	86.75	82.3	85.6	78.6
Nagaland	80.11	83.29	76.67	66.59	71.16	61.46	61.6	67.6	54.8
Sikkim	82.20	87.29	76.43	68.81	60.40	15.64	56.9	65.7	46.8
Tripura	87.75	92.18	83.15	73.19	81.02	64.91	60.4	70.6	49.7
NER	75.60			70.73					
India	74.04	82.14	65.46	64.83	75.26	53.67	51.5	63.3	38.8

Source: Census of India, 2011, Provisional Population Total, India Series-I

Table 2.7
Work Participation Rate (2001 Census)

State	*Total WPR*	*MWPR*	*FWPR*
Arunachal Pradesh	43.98	50.63	36.54
Assam	35.78	49.87	20.71
Manipur	43.62	48.12	39.02
Meghalaya	41.84	48.34	35.15
Mizoram	52.57	57.29	47.54
Nagaland	42.60	46.70	38.06
Sikkim	48.64	57.44	38.57
Tripura	36.25	50.62	21.08
India	39.10	51.68	25.63

Source: Registrar General, *Census of India.*

Religious Composition

The distribution of population can also be done in terms of the religious faiths. Indian population in terms of religion is characterised by the lopsided concentration of Hindu population followed by Muslims. These two religious groups constitute about 95 per cent of the entire population. But this pattern does not exist in the case of the NER (Table 2.8). The concentration of Hindu is highest in Tripura (85.6%) followed by Assam (64.9%), Sikkim (60.9%), and Manipur (46%). Similarly the concentration of the Christian is very high in Nagaland (90%), Mizoram (87%) and Meghalaya (70.3%) whereas the concentration of the Muslim is highest in Assam (30.9%) followed by Manipur (8.8%) and Tripura (8%) with a much smaller proportion. Typically the Buddhists are largest in Sikkim (28%). Therefore it is pretty much clear that the region accommodates different communities of people following different religious faiths.

Table 2.8
Distribution of Population by Religion, 2001 Census

	Hindu	*Muslim*	*Christian*	*Sikh*	*Buddhist*	*Jain*	*Other religions and persuasion*	*Religion not stated*
Arunachal Pradesh	34.6	1.9	18.7	0.2	13.0	0.0	30.7	0.8
Assam	64.9	30.9	3.7	0.1	0.2	0.1	0.1	0.0
Manipur	46.0	8.8	34.0	0.1	0.1	0.1	10.9	0.0
Meghalaya	13.3	4.3	70.3	0.1	0.2	0.0	11.5	0.3
Mizoram	3.6	1.1	87.0	0.0	7.9	0.0	0.3	0.1
Nagaland	7.7	1.8	90.0	0.1	0.1	0.1	0.3	0.0
Sikkim	60.9	1.4	6.7	0.2	28.1	0.0	2.4	0.2
Tripura	85.6	8.0	3.2	0.0	3.1	0.0	0.0	0.0
India	80.5	13.4	2.3	1.9	0.8	0.4	0.6	0.1

Source: Registrar General of India

Table 2.9

Crude Birth Rate (CBR), Crude Death Rate (CDR), and Infant Mortality Rate (IMR) in NER

	CBR			*CDR*			*IMR*		
State	*1991*	*2005*	*2009*	*1991*	*2005*	*2009*	*1991*	*2005*	*2009*
Arunachal Pradesh	30.9	23.3	21.1	13.5	5.0	6.1	64.5	37.0	32.0
Assam	30.9	25.0	23.6	11.5	8.7	8.4	81.0	68.0	61.0
Manipur	20.1	14.7	15.4	5.4	4.1	4.7	21.7	13.0	16.0
Meghalaya	32.4	25.1	24.4	8.8	7.5	8.1	57.0	49.0	59.0
Mizoram	17.0*	18.8	17.6	5.5*	5.1	4.5	19.0*	20.0	36.0
Nagaland	18.5	16.4	17.2	3.3	3.8	3.6	6.6	18.0	26.0
Sikkim	22.5	19.9	18.1	7.5	5.1	5.7	51.0	30.0	34.0
Tripura	24.4	16.0	14.8	7.6	5.7	5.1	56.2	31.0	31.0
India	29.5	23.8	22.5	9.8	7.6	7.3	80.0	58.0	50.0

*Relates to 1999

Source: Registrar General of India, SRS Provisional Estimates

Fertility and Mortality

One of the major concerns of the demographic dynamics is the number of births (fertility). In the absence of the external force of migration from different parts of the country or from abroad, the change of population will depend on the number of babies born. Globally the total fertility rate declined from 4.9 in 1950-55 to 2.6 in 2005-10 while during same period it moved from 6 to 2.7 in the developing countries and from 2.8 to 1.6 developed countries. At the time of independence the fertility rate in India was quite high and sticky, but, with the adoption of national family planning programme (in 1952 as the first country in the world) along with improvement in socio-economic conditions, fertility has been declining. TFR declined from 6 in 1951 to 2.6 in 2008. Table-2.9 and Table-2.10 present the evidence of the decline in demographic parameters. According to the Sample Registration System of the Registrar General of India, the birth rates of the States of the region are comparatively small. Over time since 1991 the estimates of the CBR is higher in three States of Meghalaya, Assam and Arunachal Pradesh but lower in the rest of the other region than the national average. This indicates a very healthy sign that the women in the region do not produce too many children. The national population policy also aims at a consistent level of fertility at replacement level (TFR=2.1). With this level of fertility it is assumed that after one generation the population of India will be able to stabilise. Keeping the pace and urgency of this desired goal of national population policy all the States are also trying to comply with the national targets. Whether the targets will be achieved at the stipulated time is a concern but the States also need to try to adhere to the national goals.

Given this premise, it is further shown in Table-2.10 the level of fertility in terms of the total fertility rate (TFR) and total wanted fertility rate. The national level estimate of SRS does not provide the information on the total fertility rate of the smaller States. The alternative source is the national family health survey (NFHS) which has completed three consecutive rounds conducted during 1992-93, 1998-99 and 2005-6. These rounds of survey have provided valuable data of the NER States. Being survey based, the estimated values changed from one round to another but there is a consistency of estimates from the second to third round. The estimates of the TFR from the second round to the third round show a steady decline of the demographic parameters in these States. But there is another consistency that the level of TFR in majority of the States of NER is higher than the national average.

Table 2.10

Total Fertility Rate and Wanted Total Fertility Rate in the NER

States	*NFHS-1*	*NFHS-2*	*NFHS-3*	*Wanted TFR*
Arunachal Pradesh	4.25	2.52	3.03	2.3
Assam	3.53	2.31	2.42	1.8
Manipur	2.76	3.04	2.83	2.3
Meghalaya	3.73	4.57	3.8	3.1
Mizoram	2.3	2.89	2.87	2.7
Nagaland	3.26	3.77	3.74	2.7
Sikkim	-	2.75	2.02	1.2
Tripura	2.67	1.87	2.22	1.6
India	3.39	2.85	2.68	1.9

Source: International Institute of Populations Sciences, Mumbai, NFHS-1, 2 & 3

The current fertility rate depicted by TFR is an outcome of the weighted average of all the age specific fertility rates. So it is pertinent to understand from which age fertility is having the highest impact. As presented in Figure-9 fertility begins early in Tripura, Assam, Mizoram and Arunachal Pradesh. In Assam, Arunachal Pradesh, Tripura, Sikkim and Mizoram fertility is peaked at age 20-24 while age 25-29 is peak for reproduction in Manipur, Nagaland, and Meghalaya. The age at marriage for females in the later three States is relatively late resulting into starting of reproductive life late. It is also shown that in Nagaland and Meghalaya high fertility continues till age 35-39, otherwise fertility sharply declines by age 35 in the rest of the region.

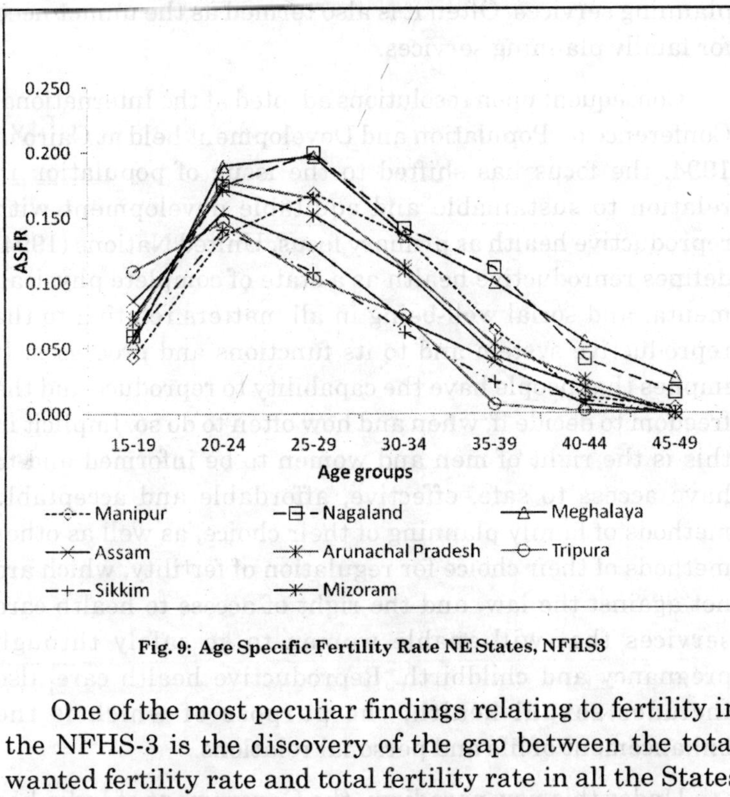

Fig. 9: Age Specific Fertility Rate NE States, NFHS3

One of the most peculiar findings relating to fertility in the NFHS-3 is the discovery of the gap between the total wanted fertility rate and total fertility rate in all the States and so the country. It shows a clear logical conclusion that all the children born to the women are not wanted or in other words there are pregnancies which are not anticipated or mistimed which resulted into a live birth. This implies that there is still some scope to reduce the current level of fertility to the wanted level. For instance, Table-2.10 vividly shows that Nagaland had the wanted TFR of three children (2.7) compared to four children being born (3.7) whereas women of Mizoram did not have much difference between what they wanted and what actually they are having (2.7 vs 2.87). From family planning programme point of view, this can be termed as mismatch of the demand for and supply of family planning services. Often it is also termed as the unmet need for family planning services.

Consequent upon resolutions adopted at the International Conference on Population and Development held at Cairo in 1994, the focus has shifted to the issue of population in relation to sustainable and equitable development with reproductive health as primary focus. United Nations (1994) defines reproductive health as a state of complete physical, mental and social well-being in all matters relating to the reproductive system and to its functions and processes. It implies that people have the capability to reproduce and the freedom to decide if, when and how often to do so. Implicit in this is the right of men and women to be informed and to have access to safe, effective, affordable and acceptable methods of family planning of their choice, as well as other methods of their choice for regulation of fertility, which are not against the law, and the right of access to health-care services that will enable women to go safely through pregnancy and childbirth. Reproductive health care also includes sexual health, the purpose of which is the enhancement of life and personal relations.

Under this new paradigm, the Government of India has also introduced the reproductive health programme

(Reproductive and Child Health, RCH) in the country since 1995. Under this the country has witnessed a lot of change in the family welfare programme which is known as paradigm shift. In one of them, the emphasis has shifted from the top-down and target fixing approach one to the informed choice of the family planning methods and demand driven mode with the feedback from the common people through the community needs assessment approach. The delivery of the programme is now executed through the National Rural Health Mission launched in 2005 in the rural areas.

It is also equally important to digest the current practice of family planning methods within marriage. Family planning methods can be of two types, such as the modern scientific methods including sterilisation as terminal method and spacing methods comprising of pills, intra uterine devices (IUD), condom, injectable and other less popular spermicides. Besides the modern methods, there are also other traditional methods which have less efficacy and effectiveness. As a result focus is given on the modern methods of either spacing or terminal. At the country level, the contraceptive prevalence rate stands at 48.5% while 7.8% are still using the traditional methods. In the region, the acceptance of traditional methods is very high particularly in Manipur, Assam and Tripura (Figure-10). If the use of traditional methods is considered, the contraceptive prevalence rate is comfortably high. If only the modern methods are considered then the prevalence rate is high in Mizoram, Sikkim and Tripura. Here we must remember that there is already unmet need for family planning services in these States. Now the question is about the motivation to use the contraceptive and regular and uninterrupted availability of the services by the providers. Availability of services is assured by the RCH programme as a flagship programme under national rural health mission in the rural areas.

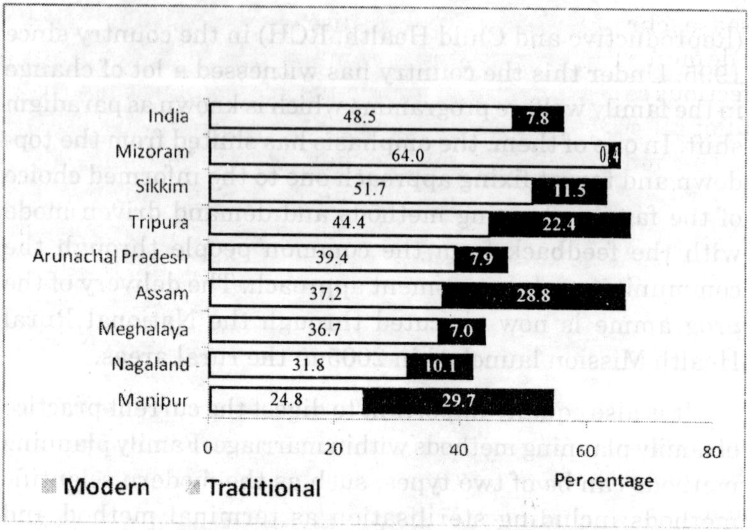

Fig. 10: Current use of contractive by modern and traditional method, NER, NFHS-3

The second half of the twentieth century saw a major decline in mortality globally, and especially in Developing Countries. Globally, life expectancy at birth for the whole population was estimated to have risen from 47 years in 1950–55 to 67 years in the current period, 2005–10, but in Developing countries as a whole this rose from 41 years to 65 years, an improvement of 24 years over half a century. Despite the fact that there were also improvements in mortality in the developed world, including further improvements in infant and child health, it seemed that the mortality gap between developed and developing countries is being gradually narrowed.

In terms of the cause of death there exist different patterns of causes observed across the world between the developed and developing countries. In high-income countries more than two-thirds of all people live beyond the age of 70 and predominantly die of chronic diseases: cardiovascular disease, chronic obstructive lung disease, cancers, diabetes or dementia. Lung infection remains the only leading infectious cause of death. In middle-income countries, nearly half of all people live to the age of 70 and chronic diseases are the major killers, just as they are in high-income countries. Unlike in high-income countries, however, tuberculosis and road traffic accidents also are leading causes of death in developing countries. In low-income countries less than a quarter of all people reach the age of 70, and more than a third of all deaths are among children under 14. People predominantly die of infectious diseases: lung infections, diarrhoeal diseases, HIV/AIDS, tuberculosis, and malaria. Complications of pregnancy and childbirth together continue to be leading causes of death, claiming the lives of both infants and mothers.

Migration

Migration, as mentioned above, is a significant factor to influence population change. It involves the permanent movement of individuals or groups of people from one place to another by crossing administrative boundaries or political boundaries. According to the Human Development Report, 2009 of United Nations Development Programme, nearly 740 million people were internal migrants mainly for the purpose of establishing a new residence and one fourth was international migration involving emigration – people moving out of the country- and immigration – people coming into the country. As many as 115 million international migrants belonged to the developed countries accounting three per cent of the world population and about 77 million international migrants lived in developing countries (United Nations, 2009). Generally, migration has been found due to 'pull' of individual or groups because of attractions of better employment avenues, political or religious freedom and 'push' of individuals or groups to move to new place for the purposes of economic or political or religious reasons. Unfortunately, unauthorized and unregulated migration has been a cause of concern to many countries, of which illegal immigration is a serious one as every country of the world aspires to control migration for maintaining domestic requirements.

Most of the ethnicities of the NER can trace their ancestries and affinities to the South-east Asia and China and also parts of mainland India in the west. These early migrants are the natives of this region. The historical events and kingdoms in different parts of mountain regions and river valleys of the eight States as witnessed by the human habitations are the bases of civilization as we see today.

It is learnt that Muslims migrated to Assam from the 13th century from North-India and later from the erstwhile East Bengal (Bangladesh). Earlier migrants assimilated themselves with the local culture and developed close societal relations with Assamese Hindus. In Manipur, Muslims appeared in the 15th century and before that Hindu Brahmins from the Gangetic plains migrated to the State. The situation of immigration is much more complex in the NER, which was at one time a distant place to the world. Migration to the Brahmaputra Valley, Manipur Valley, Barak Valley and other plain areas of the region at different historical periods took place in association with the activities of kingdoms.

Population shift from outside to this part of the world vividly started from 1826 owing to the avaricious economic exploitation and policy of colonial administration by fixing boundaries of new territories. The British colonial rulers imported people to facilitate the commercial exploitation of the new area. Adivasi and tea tribes for the new established tea gardens in Goalpara and Udalgiri areas, Assam, Muslim peasants to settle in fallow land of Assam and migrant Hindu traders from East Bengal, Rajasthan etc. as new economic avenues opened up, began to change demographic patterns of North-east India especially in Assam during the colonial regime.[30] The consolidation of colonial control over resources and commercial activities in the area were encouraged by individual traders, British entrepreneurs, adventuresome Tibetan traders and Nepali settlers. Making of rail lines, roads, modern commercial practices and a stable political situation were also the plus points for attracting migrants from the west in those colonial periods.

Population influx was more in post-colonial period as evidenced by the growth of Muslim population in Assam. Bangladesh, erstwhile East Pakistan, has been the source of several million immigrants on account of environmentally induced displacement and involuntary economic migration. The growth of Muslim population resulted in their proportion rising in Assam steadily from 16.23 per cent in 1911 to 30.91 per cent in 2001. The illegal immigration of Muslims is estimated at several millions spread over the entire region. In the aftermath of partition in 1947 and the liberalization of Bangladesh in 1971, there was mass infiltration into the region. But the agitation of the All Assam Students Union on the Issue of Foreigners in 1984 seems to have served as a dampener to migration flow as reflected well by the slow growth rate of population, 18.9 per cent in 1991-2001.

In Tripura, the local population has been turned into a minority community over time by cross border migrants from Bangladesh. At the time of Independence, the State had 56 per cent of tribal population, but the proportion has been reduced to 31.05 per cent by 2001, and the immigrated Bengali Hindus became the majority population capturing political and administrative powers resulting in the marginalisation issues of the 19 tribes of the State.

[30] Uddipana Goswami (2007): *Internal Displacement, Migration and Policy in Northeastern India*, Working Paper No. 8., Washington, East West Center.

Chakma refugees in Arunachal Pradesh are a bone of contention; they are tribals of erstwhile East Bengal who had left the Chittangong Hill Tract (CHT) following riots in 1961. The influx continued even after 1964 into Tripura, Mizoram and Arunachal Pradesh. The main concentration was at Changlang district, Arunachal Pradesh with about 60,000 population. The confrontation between local people and migrated Chakmas in using of forest resources and land occupation has led to demographic, economic and political tensions.

In Mizoram, migration from Bangladesh and Myanmar is estimated at about 10,000 persons engaging mainly in manual labour. Perhaps land ownership right has not been given to them. Meghalaya is another destination of Bangladeshi migrants, who are deprived of cultivation due to poor soils of the plateau and unavailability of land at Garo, Khasi and Jaintia mountains. The migrants could easily mix up with the local people through matrimonial alliance as the society of these communities adopts matriarchy. This has brought an impact causing change of facial look and height of body of new generation especially in urban areas where access to earning means are comparatively easy.

Myanmar nationals do enter taking the advantage of ethnic affinity across the porous international boundaries. During the World War II, many persons of Indian origin fled to Manipur and other States as well. Secondly, after the Ne Win government put the Aliens Act in place in 1967, students and political activists of Myanmar began to take asylum in the region in particular. Third, repression in the Arakan Mountain Tracts in recent time has caused cross border movement of people. The immigrated Myanmerse is estimated above 12,000 persons in Mizoram.

Nepali immigrants to the region are well known. They came to the region during the colonial periods as soldiers, manual labourers, cultivators and grazers and further scaled up by the Indo-Nepal Friendship Treaty of 1950 and two other treaties in 1951 and 1956 for their settlement in various parts of the region.[31] Due to proximity and convenient of mountain topography, a heavy influx of Nepalis to Darjeeling and Sikkim areas took place. In all the eight States, Nepali population concentrate in the rural segments where they do cultivation, and rearing of cattle, etc.

Tibetan migrants to the North-east India can be traced clearly from 1960 to 1965 when hundreds of Tibetans along with Dalai Lama fled to India from the Chinese occupied Tibet to escape persecution of Chinese government. Some of them settled in Arunachal Pradesh and Sikkim. As per record, about 15,000 Tibetans took settlement in Arunachal Pradesh.

In-migration from other States of India

The second important type of migration experienced by the North-east region has been the one through the surface route crossing East Pakistan, now Bangladesh before Indian independence, and now through the narrow corridor of foothills in North-Bengal, by train as well as vehicles. Their migration is related to various socio-economic backgrounds. There is a huge shift of population consequent upon migrated population as more than one million population was recorded as net migration from the rest of India to the region in 1991-2001.Table –2.11 highlights that Assam received 5.15 lakh persons in the decade from outside the region in addition to 95,890 persons from her regional sisters States. Her demographic characteristics are very much influenced by the migrant population from Bihar, West Bengal, U.P., Rajasthan and Jarkhand receiving 172,825, 99,034, 50,142, 30,478 and

---

[31] Amarjeet Singh, M (2009): *A Study on Illegal Immigration into North East India, The Case of Nagaland*, Occasional Paper, No. 8, New Delhi, Institute for Defence Studies and Analysis (IDSA).

Table 2.11

North-East India: Migration by Birth Place, 2001

State	*Total*	*Migrated from Abroad*	*Migrated from India*	*Migrated from NE States*	*Inter-Dist. Migration*	*Intra-Dist. Migration*
Arunachal Pradesh	1,097,968	25,468	170,626	105,628	52,411	157,043
Assam	26,655,528	190,558	515,924	95,890	1,535,561	4,386,192
Manipur	2,166,788	2,148	18,529	9,337	77,736	261,982
Meghalaya	2,318,822	12,360	92,088	59,267	44,108	209,891
Mizoram	888,573	17,160	38,570	31,091	84,851	119,715
Nagaland	1,990,036	7,984	85,550	48,108	76,443	189,480
Sikkim	540,851	22,594	52,985	2,832	32,179	76,010
Tripura	3,199,203	299,813	62,890	50090	99,669	476,680
NER	38,857,769	578,085	1,037,162	402,243	2,002,958	5,876,993
India	1,028,610,328	6,166,930	42,341,703	1,096,951*	7,684,146	181,799,637

*Total migrated population from North-East States to elsewhere in India.

Source: Census of India, 2001 D-Series

17,883 persons respectively during the period. Migration of 33,504 persons from Tripura to Assam was the highest among the NER States in the decade. The rich deposits of oil, minerals and emerging regional importance of Guwahati city and its catchment areas for commercial activities, besides the fertile Brahmaputra valley, attract outsiders to the State. Arunachal Pradesh received 170,626 migrants from the rest of India during the same decade. Bihar, UP and West Bengal were leading among the States, contributing more than ten thousand each of migrant population. More than six per cent of the total population of Meghalaya in 1991-2001 was migrants, for which Assam, Bihar and West Bengal were major contributors sending more than 65 thousand population during the period.

Bihar has outnumbered other States in terms of contribution to immigrants into the region. They are present everywhere in the region for a number of economic activities such as labour works, cobbler, hair saloon, milk supplier, retail vendors, unused plastic and scrap suppliers, etc.

Migrants from India and abroad composed of 1,108,159 males and 905,176 females who are engaging in various economic works. Its ratio 1:0.8 shows potential to expand the family size which will impact on population growth and local resources. Of them 58.33 per cent concentrate in rural areas showing that those migrants are engaging in rural oriented economic pursuits.

Urbanization in the North-East States

Urbanization plays a significant role in the spatial and economic integration of social and economic system of a region. The changing form, economic base and social structure of cities and towns will continue to be significant. We are all living now in an increasingly urbanized world. The only difference is most people (70%) in developed western countries live in urban environment, while in developing countries the proportion is mostly below 40 per cent.

The urban India has been shaped up by a long urbanization process. Urbanization in the country has very ancient roots starting from the Indus Valley Civilization where agriculture was the predominant occupation. The partition of India in 1947 had a great impact on the urbanization process of all over the country. In the region, perhaps urban development started based on the subsistent peasant economy on some selected kingdoms of plain dwellers of Manipur Valley, Brahmaputra Valley, Agartala plain etc. In the region, the boost to urbanisation was given by the introduction of modern infrastructure and other amenities during the British occupation. By way of making the head quarters at Shillong, exploitation of resources like tea and oils in Assam and war strategic features, the Britishers created many urban nucleus mainly in Assam, Meghalaya, Manipur, Nagaland and Tripura.

The process of urbanization in the region appears to have been restricted to the administrative centres and the valleys. Many of the urban centres of the region are outgrown villages which had developed to the urban centres of low size class. Out of 254 urban centres in 2001, 233 towns belong to towns of less than 50,000 population. Because of the proliferation of such small towns in mountains and plains, the number of towns has increased from 30 to 254 during 1951-2001. In the case of class I, the region has recorded 10 in 2001, with high degrees of primacy over other towns. Guwahati with more than 8 lakh population was leading, followed by Shillong urban agglomeration (UA) with 2.67 lakh population and Imphal UA with 2.5 lakh population. It is clear that Guwahati has emerged as a regional centre. In the hierarchy of urban centres, class II categories of towns in North-east like Bongaigaon, Karimgunj, Kohima, Tura etc, numbering 11 are significant as links between the higher order urban centres and the lower order ones.

Mizoram has been the highest urbanized State in the region in 2001 with 49.50 per cent share of urban population followed by Manipur with 23.88 per cent, which is of course below the national average. As revealed in Table –2.12, the lowest was Assam with 12.90 per cent but she contributed more than 50 per cent of the region's total urban population. Altogether, the region contributed 3 per cent to the total urban population of the country.

Table 2.12
North-East India: Urban Sharc of thc Population, 1951-2001

(Figure in %)

State	*1951*	*1961*	*1971*	*1981*	*1991*	*2001*	*% Change over 1991-2001*
Arunachal Pradesh	0.00	0.00	3.7	6.56	12.80	20.75	101.57
Assam	4.6	8.4	8.9	9.88*	11.10	12.90	31.64
Manipur	0.50	8.7	13.2	26.42	27.52	26.28	11.54
Meghalaya	9.66	15.3	14.6	18.07	18.60	19.58	36.02
Mizoram	3.54	5.4	11.4	24.67	46.10	49.63	38.70
Nagaland	NA	5.2	10.0	15.52	17.21	17.23	69.53
Sikkim	NA	NA	NA	16.14	9.10	11.07	61.81
Tripura	6.67	9.0	10.4	10.99	15.30	17.06	28.76
Total NER	NA	NA	NA	16.74	13.83	15.66	33.52
India	17.60	18.4	19.9	23.34	23.71	27.82	31.13

* Projected figure as no Census of Assam in 1981

Source: i) Census of India, 1991, Paper-1, Provisional Totals, 1992
ii) Basic Statistics of NER, NEC, Shillong, 2008

Objectives of NPP

The immediate objective of the NPP 2000 is to address the unmet needs for contraception, health care infrastructure, and health personnel, and to provide integrated service delivery for basic reproductive and child health care. The medium-term objective is to bring the TFR to replacement levels by 2010, through vigorous implementation of inter-sectoral operational strategies. The long-term objective is to achieve a stable population by 2045, at a level consistent with the requirements of sustainable economic growth, social development, and environmental protection.

National Socio-Demographic Goals for 2010

(1) Address the unmet needs for basic reproductive and child health services, supplies and infrastructure.

(2) Make school education up to age 14 free and compulsory, and reduce drop outs at primary and secondary school levels to below 20 per cent for both boys and girls.

(3) Reduce infant mortality rate to below 30 per 1000 live births.

(4) Reduce maternal mortality ratio to below 100 per 100,000 live births.

(5) Achieve universal immunization of children against all vaccine preventable diseases.

(6) Promote delayed marriage for girls, not earlier than age 18 and preferably after 20 years of age.

(7) Achieve 80 per cent institutional deliveries and 100 per cent deliveries by trained persons.

(8) Achieve universal access to information/counselling, and services for fertility regulation and contraception with a wide basket of choices.

(9) Achieve 100 per cent registration of births, deaths, marriage and pregnancy.

(10) Contain the spread of Acquired Immunodeficiency Syndrome (AIDS), and promote greater integration between the management of reproductive tract infections (RTI) and sexually transmitted infections (STI) and the National AIDS Control Organisation.

(11) Prevent and control communicable diseases.

(12) Integrate Indian Systems of Medicine (ISM) in the provision of reproductive and child health services, and in reaching out to households.

(13) Promote vigorously the small family norm to achieve replacement levels of TFR.

(14) Bring about convergence in implementation of related social sector programs so that family welfare becomes a people centred programme.

In order to achieve the objectives and goals 12 strategic themes have been framed for implementation. Besides this, there has been provision for constituting the national commission on population as well as State commission on population supported by various ministries for a successful integration of the programmes and coordination for implementation of such programmes. However, no attempt has been seen in the region for evolving State level population policies.

3

Society and Culture of Manipur

—M.C. Arun

The State of Manipur is homeland to various ethnic groups. The Meitei is the majority group and non-tribal. Thirty three ethnic groups are recognized as Scheduled Tribes in India. A few tribes are not yet recognized as Scheduled Tribes. All the languages of indigenous ethnic groups belong to the Tibeto-Burman linguistic family. Among them, only the Meitei has script and a recorded history since first century AD. Many ethnic groups speaking languages of Indo-European linguistic family are also in Manipur. Majority of them reached Manipur during colonial period as businessmen, security personnel, and administrative staff. These newly arrived groups were mainly from mainland India and Nepal.

Due to various social and political factors, ethnic fusion and fission take place in the State; and hence, new ethnic identities are formed now and then. This process of ethnic fusion and fission has been taking place since early days. Because of this process, new ethnic groups are formed. The Meitei is one of such ethnic group that had been formed out of ethnic amalgamation and the Meitei culture was formed out of long interactions of various ethnic groups. But, a thread of unity of these ethnic groups is obviously there to bind these ethnic groups.

From pre-historic times, different streams of people migrated from different directions to Manipur. Different racial groups from the east and the west reached Manipur. Many linguistic groups entered this country. They had different religious faiths. They settled in both mountain and valley regions. Out of ethnic amalgamation and cultural assimilation in the valley, a unique Meitei identity was forged by first century AD. Later, a Manipuri identity emerged bringing within its fold the Meitei and other indigenous ethnic groups of Manipur. This long historical experience and constant interaction between the Meitei and other ethnic groups brought out the emergence of Manipuri civilization.

Manipur has various topographical features. Each topographical area has its own features and different natural resources. The mountains, plains and water bodies demand different adaptation strategies of the people living there. Peoples in different ecological zones adapt to environment with different techniques. The people of the State show certain variations in the adaptation mechanism. Geographically, the mountains of Manipur are divided into two: Eastern mountain range and Western mountain ranges. There is a central valley, surrounded by the mountain ranges. However, by considering the topographical features and ethnic background of the peoples in the State together, we can classify the peoples of Manipur into four categories:

a) Northern highlanders

b) Valley dwellers

c) Lakeshore and island dwellers

d) Southern highlanders.

Northern Highlanders

The northern side of the State has an altitude of 913 m to 3114m above the mean Sea level. Almost the major rivers in the State originate from northern mountain ranges. The major ethnic groups in this part of the State are the Tangkhul, the Poumai, the Mao, the Maram, the Kabui/ Rongmei. There are the Thadou, the Liangmei, the Thangal (Koirao), Nepali and other ethnic groups, too. The Nepali villages in this zone are Kanglatongbi, Charhazar, Irang etc. Excepting the ethnic groups coming from other parts of India and the Thadou, other ethnic groups have, in pre-colonial period, village chieftainship. Every village has a chief and a village council consisting of representatives of several social groupings. These offices are generally hereditary.

The most significant characteristic feature of these northern highlander societies is their land use pattern. In these societies, though individuals do not have any permanent rights in land, there are three zones of land in which the rights-in-land are distributed uniquely. The zones are homestead land where the land belongs to individual households, lineage land where a group of households belonging to a particular lineage share the rights to use the land, and the community land where the entire village share the rights. The plots of land are distributed by the chief-in-council at interval time. The distribution of land is done at interval period of time by the chief in council. When new plots of land are given to individual households, the old plots become community property in which no individual or lineage has right in it.

Besides the shifting cultivation, many communities among the northern highlanders practice terrace cultivation at a significant level. Both the shifting and terrace cultivations are rainfed; but the terrace cultivation can hold water for a longer period of time. As the shifting cultivation shifts field in a regular interval, the dispute over land with neighboring villages is often reported.

All the ethnic groups in this geographical zone are patriarchal and patrilineal. The descent also traces down the male line. The inheritance of the parental property goes down in the male line.

The pottery traditions in the mountain areas of Manipur are found only in Oinam village of the Poumei and Nungbi of the Tangkhul. The pots made in these villages have a unique quality. Other pottery traditions in Manipur are in the Meitei villages of Thongjao, Chairel, Nongpok Sekmai and Andro; the first three villages are in the foot mountain areas of Thoubal Districts and the last one is of Imphal East District. Traditionally the pottery traditions are of handmade; they do not use wheel in making pots. In the case of Nungbi pottery, clay and black rock are the two main ingredients. It is basically a male-oriented handicraft.

The megalithic monument is one of the elements of material culture abundantly found among the northern highlanders. The megalithic cultures of the Mao, the Maram and the Poumai have a unique place in the megalithic culture of the State. Other megalithic monuments are also found in the areas inhabited by the Thangkhul, the Anal, the Kabui (Rongmei), the Laingmei, the Zemei, the Maring, the Thangal, the Koireng. Many megalithic remains are found in different parts of Manipur valley. The frequently found megalithic monument is menhirs; but other types such as cairn (with or without stone circle), dolmen, cromlech are also found in the State.

The northern highlanders have their colorful festivals of both cyclic and non-cyclic kinds. These festivals are related either with fertility, social ranking, lineage-specific, or community affairs. Some festivals are marked with the beginning of agricultural activities or harvesting. The Maram festival of Konghi festival is remarkable. The seven day customary festival is held in the month of Kanghi-kii (December). Wrestling is played during the festival in the Khullakpa's compound in stark naked to get shy away the devils so as to obviate misfortune and injury. There are several competitions among the youths of different lineages in public, too.

Laonii is one of the sacred festivals of the Poumai. It is celebrated on completion of paddy transplantation in the month of July. The festival is to mark a great enjoyment after successful rice transplantation and to rejuvenate their mind and health after hard work in rice transplantation. During the festivals, many socio-religious activities take place. It ranges from juvenile activities to naming ceremony of newborns. Visitors from other villages are welcome and are given hospitalities in the festival days.

In the lunar month (December-Janurary), the Kabui/ Rongmei celebrates the festival of Gang-Ngai for five days. The festival starts with honoring their ancestors through rituals. It is full of community feasts, various programs of music and dance performances.

Another colorful festival in the northern highland is the Chumpha festival of Tangkhul. The festival is celebrated for seven days after harvesting. It lasts for seven days. In this festival women play a special role. The festival is associated with community feast, gatherings and rejoicing. On the last day of the festival, there is a procession within the village boundary.

Valley dwellers

Surrounded by mountains and mountains, a small area of 1843 sq kms is the Manipur valley (including the lakeshore and island areas). The valley slopes down towards the south. Many rivers pass through this valley making it fertile. These rivers make the unique environment of the valley for various economic activities. It is only the Manipur valley where the Manipur Land Reform and Land Revenue Act 1956 is extended. The land record is maintained only for the entire valley and a small portion of mountains districts. The transfer of landed property is done only in accordance with the provisions of this Act. Hence, there is more or less permanent rights-in-land of individuals.

There are various ethnic groups in the valley region. Though there is a segregation of settlements along the ethnic line in the valley, the organic bond of different settlements is obviously found in this region. In the valley region, there are pockets of peoples coming from other parts of India. Among them the settlements of Bihari, Nepali and Bengali are prominently seen. Nepali settlements are larger comparatively than those of other Indian groups. Among the settlements of other indigenous groups, the Kabui settlements are widely distributed throughout the length and breadth of the valley.

Among the valley dwellers, the Meitei is majority group. There are three numerically sizeable different religious groups among the Meiteis: Hindu Meitei, Meitei embracing traditional religion and the *Pangan* (Muslims). There are Meitei Christians too; they are minority among the Meiteis. The Meitei Hindus are numerically superior to other religious groups. The Meitei Hindu society has only two castes, viz., the *Bamon* (Manipuri Brahmin) and the *Kshetriya* (ordinary Meitei). The other two varnas, the *Vaishya* and the *Sudra*, are not found in the society. There are exterior castes, collectively known as *Loi*. However, the lineage names cannot be sole criteria of one's caste affiliation as lineage names are distributed across the caste lines. The *Bamon* and the *Pangan* are outside the *Yek* (clan) system of the Meitei which is prevailing among the *Kshetriyas* and Meitei following traditional religion. The *Yek* system of the Meitei covers the

Loi too. There are seven *Yeks* in the Meitei society, viz., Mangang, Angom, Luwang, Khuman, Moirang, Khaba-Nganba and Sharang-Leishangthem. There are many lineage name under each *Yek*. Though the Bamon and the Pangan do come under the *Yek* organization, these Meitei groups have lineage names. Some of them are common to all the Meitei groups. On the other hand, the Meitei Hindus also follow the Hindu rules of *Gotra*. *Gotra* governs the religious performances of all the Meitei Hindus (both the *Bamon* and the *Kshetriya*). With the synthesis of Chaitnya Vaishnavism and their traditional practices, the Meitei society could develop a new school of Hinduism called Manipuri Vaishnavism in the second half of the eighteenth century.

The central valley is otherwise fertile valley as many rivers provide an environment of soil fertility. The Imphal River flows from the north towards south. It is originated from Bolenpat, near Kangpokpi. Iril, Thoubal, Chakpi, Khuga, Kongba and Sekmai rivers are important tributaries of the Imphal River. The area contains high nutrient supply derived from riverine systems. The people dwelling in this area generally practice wet-cultivation. The fields are not only rain fed but also well irrigated. Unlike in the mountainy zones where *hoe* is main agricultural implement for tilting soil, the valley agriculturalists use modern technology in tilting soils, beside their traditional plough and yoke. The bulls are used in tilting and leveling soils for preparation of seed sowing. As the staple food of the people of Manipur is rice, they cultivate paddy in major portion of their cultivating fields. In the off-season, they also cultivate various cash crops and vegetables.

As the peoples in the central valley region could drain out and manage the water bodies, swampy areas, a new society was formed out of the interactions of various ethnic groups in this area. After a gradual change in their polity, a centralized political authority emerged. The fertile soil, surplus production, advanced technology, high density of population along with the impact of people's movement on the ancient trade route helped the process of state formation in the valley. Thus, the Meitei established their state in first century AD. As this valley is at the ancient trade route connecting China and India (and beyond), various cultural elements of the East and the West met here. Synthesizing these elements, the people of this state could develop a civilization. The state thus evolves to become the present political identity of Manipur. There were, in the pre-modern period, various political functionaries at the level of *Leikai* (locality), village, *Pana*. Delegation of powers from the centralized authority was customarily made.

The Meitei society has a long literary history. Scholars of different fields maintained wrote various texts, collectively known as *puya*. In these *puyas*, the accumulative knowledge of the people of this state through ages were recorded, discussed or analyzed. These *puyas* reflect the historical experiences of the people of Manipur and how these experiences brought changes in their collective ideas.

In the first quarter of 18th century, the Meitei society became a Hindu society with which the caste hierarchy was introduced. Earlier many Hindu elements reached Manipur and had been absorbed in the society discreetly; but in the 18th century, the Hindu elements had been synthesized with traditional elements. One of the notable religious experiences of the Meitei is the existence of traditional religion along with their newly adopted Hinduism. The Meitei religious system has two independently operate systems of traditional religion and Manipuri Hinduism. A Hindu Meitei worships, performs rites and rituals of both religions as the religious situation demands. Beside the Hindu gods and deities, a Meitei still believe in their traditional and historically deep rooted gods, deities, Umang Lai and evil forces. Moreover, Meitei society has two sets of religious specialists who would perform rites and rituals in their respective sphere.

In the 18th century, Meitei society changed religious belief twice. King Pamheiba (1709-1748) converted the society to Ramanandi school of Hinduism in 1725. The society again changed its religious system to Chaitanya School of Vaishnavism during the reign of King Bhagyachandra (1759-1762, 1763-1798). The new cultural experiments during the 18th and 19th century could bring out their unique religious performances such as *Raas Lila, dhumèn, khubak ishei, lairik haiba thiba*. In these performances, there is strong blending of traditional elements and Hindu themes. This gave birth to a set of new texts of religious performance in the state.

Likewise, the Pangan (Manipuri Muslim), a part society of the Meitei, gave birth of new performances, cultural texts by blending the Meitei traditions and Islamic theme. Many folksongs of different genre, their contribution in Meitei textile industry, music and musical instruments are remarkable contributions towards the total Manipuri civilization. Such blending of different cultural sets is also seen in various festivals among the *Pangans*.

Lakeshore and island dwellers

There are 155 wetlands in the State covering about 2.1% of its total geographical area. Almost all of the wetlands are in the central valley. Some of the notable wetlands are Ikop, Waithou, Ngarka pat, Loushipat, Leingangpat, Laphupat, Laikoipat, Kharungpat and Loktak. Loktak is largest freshwater lake not only in the State but also in the entire region of North East India. It has an area of 28,700 ha. There are about 55 rural and urban settlements in and around the Loktak Lake.

These fishermen can be of three categories: island communities that command about 8300 fishermen, lakeshore communities having around 40,500 fishermen and *phum* dwellers of about 1600 fishermen. *Phum* is floating vegetations on which huts are built for fishing purposes. Earlier these huts were built temporarily. These days, due to economic pressures, these *phum* houses become more or less permanent.

The lakeshore and island dwellers are predominantly the Meitei. But, occupationally, they are different from Meiteis of other parts of the State. Majority of these dwellers engage in fishing activities. Beside the Meitei villages, there are a few Kabui villages in this zone.

There are four islands in tho Loktak Lake. They are Thanga, Karang, Sendra and Ithing. Thanga, largest island, conists of two "islet mountainocks – Thanga Chingjao and Thanga Wangma Ching, the two being disconnected by a relatively wide channel. The Thanga community is a part society in a larger Meitei society. This group is more or less endogamous group having their place in the caste hierarchy of the Meitei. They were one of the *Loi* groups in historical times.

Some of notable villages where Thanga-origin inhabitants migrated out are Keibul, Chingmei, Keirenphabi, Thanga Lawai, Khordak, Nongmaikhong, Tera and Tokching (in Pumlen lake). They have also settled side by side with other sections of the Meiteis in villages like Imphal, Sandangkhong, Ithai, Kumbi, Moirang Khunou, Moirang, Phubala, Ningthoukhong, Komlakhong, Mayang Imphal etc.

Moirang and Mayang Imphal are on the lakeshore of Loktak Lake. These towns were ancient seats of power for Moirang clan and for Khuman clan respectively. They have contributed significantly to the emergence larger Meitei polity. Moirang's lore, different narratives, textiles enriched the larger Meitei culture.

In the lakeshore areas, the peoples engage in both the fishing and cultivation. They develop many fishing techniques and boat designs to suit the changing lake surface. They also engage in wet cultivation. Today, many commercial farming grows up. The dwellers make ponds around the lake shores. The traditional reciprocal relations between the fishing community and fish traders are no longer in existence. Because of the market pressure and the individualization of fishing among the fishermen, many easily available methods are employed to catch more fishes without considering much about the ecological and cultural norms.

As the water level is now kept at a higher level throughout the year, new improvised *phum* fishing is used currently in the Loktak Lake. This is called *Athaphum* (cultivated *phum*). It is practiced throughout the year and throughout the Lake, mainly in the central zone of the Lake. It is practiced these days in order to adapt to changing socio-economic and ecological conditions is *Athaphum*. Once, it was only traditional practice of *phumdi* fishing that the communities employed.

Southern highlanders

Mountains in the southern part of the State are not very high from mean sea level. The ethnic groups inhabiting in this area are the Thadou, the Paite, the Hmar, the Anal, the Maring, the Moyon, the Monshang, the Vaiphei, the Aimol etc. The Thadou, constituting about 5 per cent of the State population, are scattered in different ecological zones of the State. But, their majority population is found in this area. Majority of the Hmars are in two blocks of Churachandpur Districts, namely, Tipaimukh and Churachandpur. The Maring and the Anal are mainly in Tenoupal Subdivision of Chandel District. The Moyon, the Monsang, the Aimol, the Chothe/Purum, the Kom inhabit in the footmountain areas of this zone.

Among the Thadou, the Vaiphei, the Hmars, there is no kinship group above the lineage. There is no exogamous kin group above the family. But, in the societies of the Moyon, the Monsang, the Anal and the Aimol, the system of moiety is prevailing. In a moiety system, the society is divided into two exogamous groups. Marriage within a moiety is prohibited. A man should marry a girl of the other moiety. Unlike other moiety systems, the Aimol moiety has a hierarchy: one moiety is considered superior to another. The division of the ethnic groups into three exogamous units is found among the Tarao and the Lamgang. In these societies, the exogamous units having lineages and other kin groups are arranged. Bride price is found in many societies among the southern highlanders. A bride price is otherwise known as bride wealth. It is an amount of money or property paid by the groom or his family to the parents of the bride.

Shifting cultivation is common form of agricultural activities among the southern highlanders. The land is usually belonged to the village chief and his council. Absolute ownership of land by the chief is found among the Thadou, the Zou and the Paite. The chief usually distribute plots of land for shifting cultivation every year. The ethnic groups of southern highlanders who dwell at the footmountain areas do also practice wet-cultivation. The plots where they practice wet-cultivation are privately owned by the individuals. These lands are generally within the purview of Manipur Land Reform and Land Revenue Act. Some of the ethnic groups who practice both shifting cultivation and wet cultivation are the Chiru, the Chothe/Purum, the Kom, the Monsang, the Moyon. The plots of shifting cultivation are allotted to individual or individual household by the chief; the villagers share a fixed amount of their agricultural products to the chief. They also work free in the cultivating field of the chief one day.

In all the societies of this area, the patriarchal and patrilineal are the thumb rules. The inheritance of property is through male line only. No woman can inherit any parental property. The Thadou inheritance is also through male line. If no male issue is there, the property and other rights are passed down to his brothers (according to birth order). The heir will have to accept any liability to the deceased and repayment of the debts are his duty. If he has son, then his property will be inherited by his son. The titles, offices, chieftainship and headship of a family are passed down to eldest son of the deceased. However, the parental house is given to the youngest son.

4

History and Polity

—N. Joykumar Singh & S. Mangi Singh

History

Manipur is the homeland of various ethnic groups of people and dialects. However, the origin of the people of the land is still quite obscure. Many writers have advanced different theories from various perspectives. It is said that the Manipuris were the descendants of the Tartar colony (Pemberton). R. Brown said, "although the general features amongst them, none of them showing regularly approaching the Aryan type". It is also suggested that the Manipuris were descended from the surrounding tribes than from the Tartar Colony from China (W. McCulloch). From the basis of the linguistic point of view some writers was of the view that there is a combined appellation of the Siamese Tai and in the Kachin Chinese 'Moy' in the name 'Moitay' of Manipur. In the midst of these differences of opinion, there is an accepted view that linguistically Manipuris are the most advanced section of the Kuki - Chin people and their language belongs to the Tibeto-Burmans group and so they are of the same family with the group.

In the early period, Manipur was known by different names. The Burmese called her as 'Kathe', the Cacharis as

'Monglai' and the people which inhabited in the surrounding area of Ningthee rivers such as Shans and other group of people called her 'Cassay'. Even some writers make a serious attempt to identify the name of this place with the Manipur of Mahabharata. But this theory was not accepted due to the complete absence of proper historical evidences. The present name Manipur as mentioned in the ancient texts was known only in 18th century with the emergence of Hindu religion concept in the area. Apart from these, there were also other names of this place. From this it may not yet be possible to identify the exact name of this place at every stage of her history, and this requires further research.

Like other countries Manipur also had a lot of evidences about the pre and proto-history culture and civilization. The reconstruction of pre history depends on the source materials like stone, bone tools and weapons, potteries, plants and animal remains. Such type of pre-historic cultural objects were also discovered in Manipur and these objects had provided bases to the historians and archaeologists in the process of re-construction of stone age, both Paleolithic (old) and Neolithic (New), and culture of this place. But due to the need of large scale research work in this area, still the historians are not yet able to give a comprehensive picture of the pre-historic culture and life of the people of this place. The Khangkhui caves in the Ukhrul district, the Tharon caves in Tamenglong district and Napachik of Thoubal district are some of the good evidences of the existence of culture and society of the pre and proto history periods of Manipur.

Though there were many references to the existence of rulers in the pre-Nongda Lairen Pakhangba period, yet the information and evidences are very sketchy. Actually the early history of Manipur is more or less proto-historical in nature. Some ancient texts which are treated as the chronicles and genealogies of the clan have mentioned the names of the rulers who ruled Manipur in different ancient time periods. According to these texts 'Kangba' is claimed to be the first king of this place. He was succeeded by his first son Koikoi who was popularly known as Moriya Phakalcha or Maliya Phabalcha. He was succeeded by Kaksuba. The other rulers were Tonkonba, Pitinykoi, Lamcicha, Soipaiba, etc. But due to the lack of intensive research work we are not yet able to discover the historical evidence about the social and cultural life and geo-political conditions of the periods of pre Nongada Lairen Pakhangba.

The emergence of Ninthouja dynasty under the leadcrship of Nongada Lairen Pakhagba was a great landmark in the course of the history of Manipur. The establishment of Kingdom under his rule marked the beginning of the evolution of Meitei kingdom in this place. Before his coming as an undisputed leader there were many ethnic groups who had scattered in various parts of this place with distinctive independent political identity of their own. The major ethnic groups were Luwang, Khuman, Angom, Khaba, Nganba, Mangang, Moirang, Heirem Khunjam, Sarang Leishangthem, etc. In the course of time, these ethnic groups were assimilated into the social and cultural fabrics of the ruling dynasty in one way or the other. Indeed the establishment of a new Kingdom was an outcome of the struggle between various ethnic groups and clan chieftains in the valley. But the significant contribution towards the establishment of kingdom was the outcome of the conflict between Poireiton, a prince of Khamnung country, and Nongda Lairen Pakhangba. In this clash for the establishment of authoritative power Nongda Lairen Pakhangba came out with victory crown on his head and it led for the emergence of new political environment in this area. Then another important event was the struggle for the throne between Khaba and Nongda Lairen Pakhangba. The Khaba was the ruler of Kangla. The Khaba chief who challenged the emerging power of Nongda Lairen Pakhangba was Khaba Nongchengba. So for a pretty long time a clash was continued for the throne of Kangla between these two personalities. Finally Nongda Lairen Pakhangba killed Khaba chief and thus he became the sole undisputed leader for the throne of Kangla.

The victory over Khaba was a big turning point in the course of the history of Manipur. After hearing of the news of the victory, leaders of other ethnic groups began to extend their loyalty to the new leader. And gradually they began to assimilate in the social fabric of Ningthouja dynasty. The process of the coronation ceremony had clearly demonstrated the nature of the service rendered by the chiefs of various ethnic groups towards the new leadership. His coronation ceremony was attended by Puleiromba, the chief of Angom, Luwang Langmaiba, one Luwang priest, Ninthem Apanba, Mayang Chief. Even a large number of leaders of Chakpa also attended the function. It is also recorded that the Chakpas arranged personnel for the protection of Nongda Lairen Pakhangba and they guarded him at Kangla during the coronation ceremony. Thus, with this particular event, the process of Meitei state formation started under the leadership of Nongda Lairen Pakhangba.

Just after the consolidation of his position, Nongda Lairen Pakhangba began to pay attention towards the establishment of new system of statecraft in a more scientific way. In order to have a systematic character in the administration he created several departments. They are: (1) Laipham Sanglen, a court of justicesl (2) Kuchu Sanglan (3) Khanba Sanglen (4) Naharup Sanglen (5) Pache Loisang, court dealing with women affairs and presided over by queen Leima, wife of Nongda Lairen Pakhangba. During his period a large number of groups of people had migrated here and it created a problem for the administration. But Nongda Lairen Pakhangba very carefully handled the situation and all the migrants were allowed to make a settlement at different places of the country. Here some writers give a different version about the identity of these people, and thus leading to the controversy over the nomenclature. Besides, Pakhangba also had successfully tried to consolidate the society which was emerging gradually towards a more unified one. The acceptance of clanship by Luwang, Angom, Mangangs, Khaba, Nganbas, Sarang – Leishangthem, etc. under the political supremacy and social confederacy of Nongda Lairen Pakhangba marked the beginning of successful evolution of Meitei state formation. Thus from his reign, the course of the history of this place began to move towards a more dynamic one with a distinctive identity of Kingdom. Further the introduction of technological development during the reign of subsequent rulers had further intensified the ongoing process of the evolution of the state. Thus with the foundation of the Ningthouja dynasty, the social and political development of the society was cantered around the ruling dynasty and the whole social and political structure was transformed from tribalism to feudalism.

The middle of fifteen century was another landmark on the course of the history of Manipur. During this period the policy of expansionism and military aggrandisement, which were adopted by the subsequent rulers of the Ninthouja dynasty, was able to reach remarkable stage. Before this period the rulers had concentrated their attention only to the expansion of political influence to the surrounding mountain areas. King Kyamba was the ruler of this place during this period. Because of his exceptional talent and capabilities he is regarded as one of the greatest Kings of Manipur. He ruled this place for 1467 to 1508 A.D. During this period Manipur was able to expand her territories and political influence upto Kabaw Valley. His earlier name was Thangwai Ningthouba. But, just after getting victory over Kyang, his name was changed to Kyamba, the conqueror of Kyang. The ancient literacy texts mentioned in detail the nature of the celebration organized by Manipur after the occupation of Kabaw Valley. Accordingly the boundary of Manipur was fixed at the Mengkhong Mumgyang area. Apart from this he also defeated the Mayangs (Thongnangs). The real identity of the invading people was not known. Local writers claimed that they were the Kacharis. But others are of the view that they were the Koch people. Whatever the case, the victory over Mayang was a clear indication of the growing military power of the kingdom of Manipur. Apart from his military success king Kyamba also introduced many reforms for the betterment of administration. Reorganisation of 'pana' system by adding two more revenue units, i.e. Ahallup and Naharup, introduction of the maintenance of the royal chronicle known as the *'Cheitharol Kumbaba'* (chronology of years according to Cheithaba) and making foundation for the growth of a plural society by absorbing people coming from outside the country (foreigner) in the Meitei society was some of the special features of the period of King Kyamba. Another important development was the emergence of the influence of Hinduism by constructing the temple of Lord Vishnu. Thus the period of King Kyabma is worthy of flagging in studying the history of Manipur.

The reign of King Khagemba was also another important period in the ongoing course of the history of this place. Some writers regarded him as the illustrious ruler of the medieval Manipur. He ruled this country from 1597 to 1652 A.D. His earlier name was Sana Hihouhan Poirei Ningthouhanba. He was a great conqueror and also a great administrator and social reformer. Apart from his military expedition against the various Shan principalities in the Kabaw Valley, he also invaded inside the Chinese territory. His military campaign against China is mentioned in *Ninthourol Lambuba*. It is said that Khagemba invaded the country of Chinese barbarism in the land of the rising sun which was beyond the Chindwin River. As a mark of the victory over Khagi

(Chinese), the name of the king was also changed to Khabemba (winner over China). Khagemba also gave a severe defeat to the Kachari and Muslim invaders. But he did not treat the war captives badly. Rather he even allowed the Muslim war captives to settle in Manipur. Then during his period the fame of Manipur was expanded even to the far places of neighbouring areas. On top of this, he was also a great nation builder. During his period Khagemba brought a new picture of administration in a more systematic way. He adopted a liberal social policy by allowing all the migrants including the Brahmins to make their settlement in Manipur possible. They were given surnames according to the system of the society. He changed the title of the king as 'Lainingthou', the godly king. The system and practice of prostration was also introduced as court etiquette. He also introduced an elaborate social etiquette and rules for the performance of duties by different officials at the court. Thus with the introduction of new social rules and practices the position of the nobility was further strengthened. In short, the feudal system was perfected during his period. In addition to this he also brought a new shape in the field of technology, economic discipline, religion and literature also. With the help of all these, Khabemba was able to consolidate the political position of Manipur.

Then the beginning of 18th century again marked another significant change in the whole social and culture life of the people of Manipur. The accession of Garibniwaz as the ruler of Manipur from 1709 to 1748 A.D. was a great water shed in the entire history of this place. He was a great military conqueror and also a significant reference in the field of culture and religion. Actually Manipur was able to reach to reach the zenith of all her capabilities and developments during this period by expanding her territories inside the territories of her neighbouring countries. The introduction of process for the *sankritisation* of Manipur by introducing the 'Ramandi Cult' was the one of the biggest epoch making events of the period of King Garibniwas. In the process of making the Hindu religion as the state religion, the people had to face a lot intolerable torture both mentally and physically from the administrators. The burning of *Puya* (ancient literacy texts), the destruction of the abodes of the traditional deities (Kolu Yaikhaiba), change of the names of the mountains, rivers, lakes to the Hindu names, forcing the people to accept the way of life of new religion were some of the important features of the sanskritisation process. Thus with the forceful introduction of new religion the cultural life of the society also began to change very fast and gradually the people began to give importance to the new religion and its way of life. The sanskritisation policy of King Garibniwaz was further consolidated during the reign of King Bheigyachandra (1749 – 1798 A.D.). Propagation of Gauriya Vaisnavism, installation of the image of Govindajee in the year 1776 and introduction of Ras Leela etc. were the important religious features of his period. And it had brought a complete transformation in the social and cultural life of the people of Manipur. And from this period afterwards the influence of Bengali culture began to enter the life of the people of Manipur. Thus a long history of the cultural and religious tradition which was continued from the very ancient period of time began to close with the introduction of new religion and its way of life.

The outbreak of 'Seven Years Devastation' (*Chahi Taret Khuntakpa*) in the year 1819 A.D. was also another epoch making event in the history of Manipur. This particular event laid the foundation for the establishment British colonial administration in Manipur. The invasion and occupation of Manipur by Burma for seven years, i.e. from 1719 to 1826 A.D. is popularly known in Manipur as the period of Seven Years Devastation. During the rule of the Burmese administration the people of Manipur had suffered a lot from the ill-treatment of the Burmese officials and soldiers. So to get themselves free from the clutches of Burma, many people fled the place and took shelter in different areas of neighbouring countries. Such type of devastating situation was saved by Gambhir Singh and Nara Singh with the help of British East India Company.

As a part of the preparation for the liberation of Manipur, they established a militia force called the 'Manipur Levy' and it was trained by British. In the meantime, British also declared war against Burma. Then with the able leadership of Gambhir Singh, Manipur was again liberated from the hand of Burma in the year 1826. Officially the First Anglo-Burmese War also came to an end with the signing of Treaty of Yandaboo in the year 1826. After this the importance of British in every aspect of the administration of Manipur began to appear. The office of the British Political Agency was established in Manipur in 1835. And this office began to act as a kind of communication line between Manipur and British. But in reality it became a very important place from where the British could exercise their influence in the day to day administration of the Kingdom. The ultimate result of the consistent interference and influence of the British came to light in 1891. The outbreak of the Anglo-Manipur War in this year was the end of the existence of Manipur as a sovereign kingdom since the time of Nongda Lairen Pakhangba in 33 A.D. In this war, Manipur was defeated and immediately colonial administration was established. Thus from 1891 to 1947 Manipur was under the colonial administration of the British. During this period the people of this place had an opportunity to witness the activities of various types of movements which were launched under the banner of different objectives. The First Women's Agitation of 1904, the Kuki Rebellion of 1917-1919, the Zeliangrong movement of 1930-32, the Second Women's Agitation of 1939, etc. may be mentioned as some significant activities involving the participation of the masses. Then from the first quarter of the 20th century the idea of political consciousness began to develop in the State. The birth of Nikhil Hindu Manipuri Mahasabha in 1934 may be observed as a great landmark towards the growth of idea of national consciousness among the people of Manipur. This body was basically a socio-religious organization. But it laid a basic foundation for the growth of political consciousness among the people and also for the birth of political party. The first political party came into being in 1938. The name of the party was Nikhil Hindu Manipur Mahasabha. The basic objective of the party was to establish a responsible government in Manipur based on the democratic principle. Thus with the establishment of the party for the first time, the people began to witness the political activities which asked for the establishment of a new system of administration within the framework of democracy. In the meantime the World War II broke out and it came to an end in the year 1945. Just after the end of the war, everybody began to feel that the independence of India was also a signal that Manipur's freedom from the hands of colonial administration was not very far. Accordingly all the political parties started to work very hard for the establishment of a democratic institution in Manipur. On the 15th of August 1947 Manipur got independence from British and the responsibilities of the administration of the State was left in the hands of King Budhachandra Singh. He was also inclined towards the establishment of a democratic form of government based on the framework of a constitution. Accordingly at the initiative of the King, the 'Manipur State Constitution Act' was passed and the 'Election Rules' was also framed to conduct the general election. The general election was held in 1948 on the basis of adult universal franchise in which no party was able to get absolute majority. Then a non-Congress coalition ministry was formed with Maharaj Kumar Priyobrata Singh as the Chief Minister. Thus, for the first time, the people were able to witness the establishment of democratic institution in Manipur, and as per the constitution the State became a constitutional monarchy.

The year 1949 was also another significant year in the entire history of Manipur. This particular year ushered the place into a new phase with the transformation from the sovereign country to a single political unit of the Indian Union. Indeed, the failure of the Congress Party to form the government in the election of 1948 was the key factor for the change of the political status of Manipur. Just after suffering defeat, they (Congress Party), in collusion with leaders of the Indian National Congress, began the open move for the merger of Manipur with the political boundary of India Union. In the course of the merger movement, the people were able to witness various types of policy and programmes adopted by the Manipur State Congress Party for having a successful integration of Manipur. Finally the Merger Agreement was signed between the Maharaja of Manipur and the Indian Government on 21st September 1949 at Shillong and it was officially announced on the 15th October of the same year. Thus with the integration of Manipur into the political boundary of Indian Union, the chapters of the history of independent Kingdom of Manipur came to an end and a new chapter was opened as a political unit of India.

Polity: Recent Trends

The entire area of the State is divided into nine districts. Of these four are in the valley. They are Imphal West, Imphal East, Thoubal and Bishnupur Districts. The remaining five are in the mountains. They are Ukhrul, Chandel, Senapati, Tamenglong and Churachandpur Districts. The valley is mainly inhabited by the Meiteis who constitute an overwhelming majority of the people there, along with the Pangals or Manipuri Muslims who constitute the single largest minority community in the state. The valley also has a number of localities where different tribes reside.

The mountains of the state, on the other hand, are home to 33 officially recognized tribes. They are Aimol, Anal, Angami, Chiru, Chothe, Kabui, Kacha Naga, Koirao, Koireng, Kom, Lamkang, Maring, Maram, Mao, Monsang, Moyon, Sema, Tangkhul, Poumai, Purum, Tarao, Kharam, Gangte, Hmar, Lushai, Paite, Ralte, Simte, Sahte, Thadou, Vaiphei, Zou and Any Kuki Tribes. At present, these tribes are divided into two broad categories – the Naga and the Kuki-Chin-Mizo group of tribes. Regarding the geographical dispersal of the different tribes in the mountains of the state, Ukhrul and Tamenglong Districts are overwhelmingly dominated by the Nagas whereas Churachandpur District is overwhelmingly dominated by the Kukis-Chin-Mizo group of tribes. In the other two remaining districts, Chandel and Senapati, both Nagas and Kuki-Chin-Mizo group of tribes constitute two more or less equally effective communities there. It is important, however, to note that none of the five mountain districts are exclusively inhabited by one particular tribe or group of tribes. In fact, there are many Kuki villages in Ukhrul and Tamenglong district, more so in case of the latter. There are also many Naga villages, particularly of those Nagas belonging to the Zeliangrong group of the Naga people (a group within the Naga community) in Churachandpur District. In case of Chandel and Senapati Districts, as already mentioned, both constitute two more or less equally effective communities there. Indeed, there was one Kuki candidate each in as many as five Naga dominated Assembly Constituencies (AC) (all the three ACs of Tamenglong District, Ukhrul AC of Ukhrul District and Karong AC of Senapati District) during the last State assembly elections of 2007. The correlates between the diverse demographic features and the politics of the State are clearly evident in the profile of the various ACs.

1.b. A profile of the ACs in Manipur

At present Manipur has a unicameral legislature having

60 seats. Of these 40 seats are General seats whereas the numbers of Scheduled Tribe and Scheduled Caste seats are nineteen and one respectively. Geographically speaking, the valley and Jiri comprise 40 ACs consisting of 39 general and one SC ACs. The mountains, on the other hand, comprise 20 ACs consisting of 19 ST and one General ACs. The General AC in the Mountains is the Kangpokpi AC in the Senapati District of the State. Of the four valley Districts in the State, Imphal East has eleven ACs, Imphal West thirteen, Bishnupur six and Thoubal ten. Regarding the mountain districts, Chandel has two, Churachandpur six, Senapati six, Tamenglong three and Ukhrul three. Regarding the ethnic composition of the ACs in the 20 ACs in the mountains, all the six ACs in the Tamenglong and Ukhrul (three each) are predominantly Naga inhabited ACs whereas the six ACs in Churachandpur District are predominantly Kuki inhabited ACs. Regarding the other two remaining districts namely Chandel and Senapati, in two ACs of the former both are effective communities in the sense that the seats are keenly contested by both the communities. In case of Senapati District, three of the six ACs of the District namely Mao, Tadubi and Karong are predominantly inhabited by the Nagas whereas two of them namely Saikul and Saitu are predominantly inhabited by the Kukis. Regarding the remaining one, i.e. Kangpokpi, both Nagas and Kukis along with the Nepalis constitute three effective communities. As a result, nine ACs in the mountains always return Naga MLAs whereas another eight ACs always return MLAs belonging to Kuki-Chin-Mizo group of tribes. In the remaining three ACS there has always been stiff competition between the Nagas and the Kukis. All these mean that representation of the Nagas and the Kuki-Chin-Mizo people in the State assembly has always been a case of either 10:10 or 11:9 or 12:8 unless the Kangpokpi AC goes to a Nepali. At present the two have ten MLAs each in the State legislature. So far nine assembly elections have been held in Manipur since

she attained her Statehood (1972, 1974, 1980, 1984, 1990, 1995, 2000, 2002 & 2007).

2. Some insights into the contemporary trends in the state of politics in Manipur

A close examination of the state of politics in Manipur since she got her statehood in 1972 reveals a number significant trends emerging inside the State. Some of these are being highlighted as follows:

2.a. Trend of coalition ministries

Ours is a parliamentary polity where freedom to form associations for collective bargaining is guaranteed by the Constitution. This has provided for not only emergence of any number of political parties in our country but also the freedom for collective bargaining among political parties. As long as there is a party winning a majority of the seats in the legislative assembly, there will be no problem for that party to form the government. The problem starts when no party wins the required majority. In such a situation, the alternative is to muster up the required numbers through alliances and this leads to the formation of coalition ministries. Such governments become all the more inevitable when parties and factions proliferate, a scenario which has become a hallmark of party system in India. Indeed, at present there is a coalition ministry both at the centre and in Manipur. Earlier, we have had coalition ministries at the Centre in 1989, 1991, 1996, 1998, 1999 and 2004. Coming to Manipur, so far the State has witnessed 20 popular ministries. Out of these as many as 17 ministries have been coalition ministries. This obviously means that coalition ministries have been the norm rather than an exception. This is not surprising at all when one remembers the fact that so far no party had won a majority of the seats in any of the nine State assembly elections held.

About the stability of the coalition governments in the State one notices a huge difference between the coalition ministries which came before the 2002 assembly elections and those coalition ministries which came after that. The fact is that during the period from the first State assembly elections in 1972 to the eighth State assembly elections in 2002, there were as many as 14 coalition ministries. Compared to this the last ten years or so following the 2002 elections have witnessed only two ministries and both also happen to be coalition ministries. The first 15 coalition ministries have accounted for a little more than 20 years which means that at an average a coalition lasted for only about one year and four months only. Coming to that of the last two coalition ministries inside the State since 2002, the Secular Progressive Front (the Congress, CPI, NCP and the MSCP) led by the Congress completed the entire full term for the first time in the history of Manipur since she became a part of the Indian union. The present Secular Progressive Front which came to power in 2007 (this time with only the Congress and the CPI as coalition partners) is once again on the verge of completing another full term. This obviously means that while the coalition ministries before 2002 failed to provide a stable government for the State, the two which came after the eighth assembly elections held in 2002 have been completely stable ones.

There were various factors responsible for the failure of the coalition ministries to last long before 2002. For one, they were factions within the coalitions all the time. In other words, inter-party conflicts have been a permanent feature of the working of coalition ministries in Manipur. The coalition partners were held together by their one and only single most common desire to be in power. The coalitions were characterized by both inter-party and intra-party conflicts. This will be true with both the larger parties and small parties within the coalitions. A tendency on the part of the larger parties in the coalition to absorb the smaller one with a view to form a government on their own has also been another permanent feature of the working of coalition ministries inside the State. This, along with the inter and intra-party conflicts, often led to the split and merger of political parties thereby upsetting the status quo of political parties within the coalition ministries and bringing the coalition ministries down. All these mean that coalition politics in the State had failed to evolve in a meaningful manner. This also inevitably led to imposition of President's Rule in the State on many occasions. In fact, there have been as many as 7 occasions since statehood when the State was put under President's Rule.

2.b. Absence of meaningful and effective opposition

The present era is the era of democracy. In a democratic setup, one party or group of parties form a government and the rest become the Opposition in the legislature. Ideally speaking, the Ruling and the Opposition parties have equal responsibility for the proper functioning of the government and leading the state on the path of progress and prosperity. The word opposition is derived from the Latin word 'oppositio' which means to oppose.[32] The origin and emergence of opposition can be traced from the ancient Greece and Rome. The modern idea of parliamentary opposition, however, emerged in British Parliament. And the term opposition, when we use it in the context of parliamentary democracy nowadays, consists of all those political party or parties which as a result of the last general election did not become part of the government. It is an inseparable part of the democratic political system. The absence of oppositional institution virtually means an authoritarian or totalitarian form of government and not a democratic political system. Indeed, there can be no democratic government without opposition

---

[32] H.S. Fartyal, *op cit.*, p.1

and a responsible opposition is as important as the party in power in a parliamentarian democracy.

The role that the Opposition performs in not only a parliamentary democracy but also in any democratic system of governance is enormous. Some of the more significant of them will be those of serving as a watchdog of the rights and liberties of the people; making national debates possible on important issues facing the country; opposing those policies and programmes of the government which they may consider as being unjust, unreasonable and not in the interest of the people; offering positive counter-proposals and initiatives of its own; throwing up important and desirable policy alternatives which have not found a space among those as generated by the Ruling side; examining and scrutinising each and every policy, programme and department of the government and highlighting the mistakes and deficiencies therein; cooperating with the government in times of emergency, national calamity and disaster, etc. As such, the opposition is considered to be indispensable in a democracy. The nature and character of opposition, however, vary from one party system to another.[33] For instance, in one-party system, opposition is not allowed to exist. In two-party system, the opposition is very strong and it is the real shadow cabinet. In a multi-party system like India, the oppositions have been weak, heterogeneous and divided among them.

Coming to the scenario in Manipur, the tradition of opposition emerged in Manipur before she got merged into India in 1949. When the first democratically constituted ministry with M. K. Priyobrata Singh as the Chief Minister was formed in 1948, the Manipur State Congress was there as the Opposition. About its role in the contemporary politics

[33] S.S. Patagundi, *The Opposition in the Indian Political System* in D. Sundar Ram (ed), *Indian Parliamentary Opposition*, Volume I, New Delhi, Kanishka Publishers & Distributors, 1996, p. 221.

of the State, like in any democratic system of government, the Opposition in Manipur is expected to play an important and constructive role. However, in actual practice, its role inside the State politics is far from satisfactory and constructive. Most of the time, it remains a weak and heterogeneous group, characterised by lack of unity. They also remain divided on party lines and engaged more in the struggle for power. In a small State like Manipur, it is desirable that all parties in Opposition are well united so that they can check the working and movement of the government and provide an alternative to the people. But most of the time the relationship among parties in Opposition is not very cordial and united in and outside the assembly. They are kept either united or divided by the sole consideration of getting an opportunity to form a new government by overthrowing the existing one.

The Opposition in Manipur also usually comprises many parties having different ideologies and beliefs. It makes it difficult for them to work together in pursuit of a common agenda for the people. As a result the relation between and among the opposition parties get strained most of the time and their ability to be a responsible and effective opposition is always weakened. They come together only occasionally. Most of the time, they are busy either trying to dislodge the party in power or trying to defect from the opposition and join the ruling party. As such they also fail to provide policy alternatives to any significant extent. This also means their failure to serve as a watchdog of the rights and liberties of the people. In fact, the role of the opposition is played by the interest groups or pressure groups which exist in the form of different civil society groups inside the society rather than by the opposition parties in Manipur. It is they which try to check the moves of the government whenever the latter's actions posed a serious danger to the interests of the people, and the Opposition followed them most of the time. For instance, when the Government of India signed a cease-fire agreement with the National Socialist Council of Nagaland (NSCN) on June 14, 2001, the civil society groups reacted first and the political parties followed them. The lack of proper coordination and understanding among opposition parties on various issues also led to their failure to evolve themselves as a meaningful group and project themselves as a viable alternative to the government. As a group also they remain vulnerable to disintegration due to divisive designs of the Ruling side. This was all the more so because there were inter-party as well as intra-party conflicts within the Opposition. As a result, prior to the 2002 assembly elections, Ruling parties often succeeded in absorbing parties in Opposition.

Regarding the relationship between the Ruling and Opposition parties in Manipur, it has been characterized by elements of friendly cooperation only once in a while. Otherwise, it remained one of conflicting rivalry. There were certain issues in connection with which there were co-operation and co-ordination between them like that of the protection of the territorial integrity of Manipur, shifting of the Assam Rifles from Kangla, finding a peaceful solution to the problem of insurgency inside the State through political dialogues, etc. Apart from these few exceptions, they had diametrically opposite views on several problems confronting the State. Considering all these about the nature and functioning of the Opposition in Manipur, one may say that overall it has so far failed to evolve itself as a healthy institution of democratic practices.

2.c. Challenges to free and fair elections

Importance of free and fair elections in democracy is something that can never be overestimated. It facilitates meaningful representation of the people in matters of governance, and lends credence to freedom of political expression, freedom of speech, freedom of choice, etc. that prevails in a country. If the process of electoral politics is not conducted in a free and fair manner, no elections, however grand their scales might have been or however regularly they might have been held, would amount to much in terms of securing popular basis and legitimacy for the political system. The danger which the absence of it poses to democracy is only too evident. Keeping this in view, when one looks at the trend of electoral politics in the mountains of Manipur, one cannot help but observe the increasing pressure on the conduct of free and fair elections there. This has become a serious concern in times of local, State as well as national elections. The ADC elections of 2010 serve as a glaring example of this.

There are six Autonomous District Councils (ADCs) in the mountains of Manipur at present – Ukhrul ADC, Tamenglong ADC, Senapati ADC, Churachandpur ADC, Sadar Mountains ADC and Chandel ADC. Each of these ADCs have 24 Autonomous District Council Constituencies (ADCCs) making the total number of the ADCCs 144. The ADC Elections, 2010 were held in two phases – the first on 26 May and the second on 2 June 2010. While Churachandpur, Chandel and Sadar Councils went to poll in the first phase Ukhrul, Tamenglong and Senapati Councils went to poll in the second phase. A careful look into the elections reveals a number of interesting things. Out of the 144 ADDCs (24 each in the six ADCs), 69 candidates were elected uncontested which include 9 from Churachandpur, 12 from Sadar Mountains, 12 from Chandel, 20 from Ukhrul, 12 from Senapati and 4 from Tamenglong District Councils. In the remaining 75 ADCCs there were no candidates in 8 ADCCs, six in Senapati and two in Ukhrul District Councils. As such, polling was scheduled only in 67 ADCCs (out of a total of 144, means in less than half). These were 15 in Churachandpur, 12 in Sadar Mountains, 12 in Chandel, six in Senapati, two in Ukhrul and 20 in Tamenglong. Again, out of these 67, there was no voting turn out at all in two ADCCs (both in Senapati ADC) as the candidates in these ADCCs announced their retirement from the elections after their candidature were duly accepted by the election authorities. About the final results, overall, it was land slide victory for the Congress winning 106, IND 25, CPI 1, Trinamool 1 and NCP 1.

Regarding the pressure put on the conduct of free and fair elections, a number of significant things make it obvious. For instance, at least two Congress candidates were kidnapped there. Reports of many candidates receiving threats, telling them to withdraw their candidature and that otherwise they will face dire consequences were also there. There was also the deadline of May 17 of the year for the withdrawal of their candidature set forth by the UNC. Reports of attacks on residences of candidates who did not comply with the deadline were there. Some houses and polling stations were also burnt down. Poll personnel escorted by security personnel were also blocked from reaching their polling stations. There was that particular episode when polling officials along with security personnel were stopped from reaching their destinations by armed cadres of the NSCN (IM). All these developments created an atmosphere of uncertainty, tension and fear for the candidates as well as the voters during the time of elections, particularly in areas where the Nagas inhabited and where the Nagas and Kuki-Chin-Mizo group of people co-existed.

As a result, the government had to provide safe shelters for the candidates in the Sports Authority of India Youth Hostel and the State Youth Centre with the 2nd Indian Reserve Battalion guarding them. At one time, there were about 85 candidates taking shelter there including two women, and an overwhelming majority of them were from the Naga dominated ADCCs. According to a District Election

Commissioner report, most of the voters in his District were prevented from the exercise of their franchise right. There were reports of voters not coming out of the polling stations even after casting their votes due to fear of what may happen to them; agents inside the polling stations refusing to be photographed by the press again for the same reason; voters telling the press that they did not cast their votes as they were warned not to cast their votes; many voters standing outside their polling stations fearing to enter and entering to cast their votes only after the arrival of security personnel; etc.

It is also significant to note that a different trend was clearly there in the Kuki-Chin-Mizo dominated areas. What happened in the Naga inhabited areas was quite in contrast to what one saw in the Kuki dominated areas. For instance, the Kuki National Organization (KNO) announced three regulations for the smooth functioning of the Autonomous District Council elections in the State to ensure public peace and orderly atmosphere. It issued a strict and mandatory compliance order for all to ensure and facilitate the passage of the true spirit of democracy in the State. It also prohibited any form of canvassing of votes by using threats and intimidations or in an unruly manner in the name of any organization. Saying that booth capturing shall be dealt with seriously, the KNO also appealed to all the voters to exercise their voting right freely and without fear. Then it comes as no surprise that overall, the voting turn out in the Kuki dominated areas was considerably higher than that in the Naga dominated areas with Churachandpur and Sadar Mountains recording 90% and 75% voter turnout respectively. Compare to it, the voter turnout in Chandel, a district where both Naga and Kuki-Chin-Mizo group of people constitute two more or less equally effective communities, recorded 48.3% only.

What happened during the ADC elections, 2010 was not an isolated one. Such trends could be seen in the assembly elections in the mountains of the state and it is also emerging in the valley to some extent. If such trend continues in the electoral politics of Manipur, it will seriously endanger the emergence of healthy and meaningful democratic institutions inside the state.

2.d. Polarization of electoral politics along ethnic lines

One of the most glaring trends concerning politics in Manipur is that of the increasing polarization of electoral politics on ethnic lines. The fact is that a sense of unity and oneness among the people is a basic precondition for development in a country/State. If the people remain divided then obviously the prospects of development will also be greatly endangered. Though the 33 tribes inside the State are broadly divided into two groups, there are also tribes who would like to assert by their own tribal names or those who say they belong to neither of these two. The tendency to identify themselves as different from others has always been there right from the very beginning. However this got more pronounced as a result of the ethnic clashes during the 1990s. The factors leading to the clashes were both historical and contemporary. Without going for elaboration, it will be suffice to note that the tradition of age-old inter-village and inter tribal conflict, British policy of divide and rule, inter-village-boundary disputes, contest for exclusive ownership rights over land, demand for Sadar Mountains District, imposition of homeland taxes, quit notices served on one group by another, etc. have not only disturbed the sense of unity and oneness among the people but also have contributed to the violent clashes that claimed about 2000 lives and many more were injured. Many were also maimed for the rest of their lives. More than 500 villages were attacked and about 7,000 houses were burnt down to ashes. It also led to the displacement of about 15,000 families and more than one lakh people. It has been against the backdrop of such a historical as well as contemporary socio-political setting that polarization of electoral politics on ethnic lines has taken place.

Now the polarization of electoral politics in the mountains of Manipur can be examined at two levels – 1) at the level of the formation of political parties there, and 2) at the level of casting votes by the people there in time of elections. About the first, most of the mountain based parties remain mostly confined in either Naga dominated or Kuki Chin dominated areas. This can be authenticated by taking up some of the important regional parties that have emerged in the mountains.

The Kuki National Assembly and the State Assembly Elections

The Kuki National Assembly is one of the oldest political parties emerging from the mountains of Manipur. However, it remains more or less exclusively confined to the Kuki-Chin-Mizo (KCM) tribes dominated areas. This can be seen from the following details about the ACs the party contested during the state assembly elections:

- 1974 elections: put up candidates in 6 ACs, 3 in Kuki-Chin-Mizo dominated ACs two in Naga dominated and another in an evenly poised AC, and won in two KCM dominates ACs (Saikul, *Saitu & Saikot,* Karong, Tadubi and Kangpokpi).
- 1980: Put up in seven, Five KCM dominated ACs and two evenly contested ACs and won in the two evenly contested ones (Saikul, Saitu, Henglep, Saikot, Singhat, *Chandel & Tengnoupal*).
- 1984: Put up in four, two KCM dominated, one Naga dominated and one evenly poised and won in one which is KCM dominated (Saitu, *Churachandpur,* Tamei and Chandel)

- 1990: Contested in eight, six KCM dominates and two evenly poised, and won in two KCM AC (Saikul, Saitu, Henglep, Churachandpur, *Saikot & Singhat,* Chandel, Tengnoupal)

- 1995: Contested in six, all KCM dominated and won in none (Chandel, Tipaimukh, Thanlon, Henglep, Churachandpur, Saikot)

- Contested in one KCM dominated AC – Siakot but again won in none.

It is obvious from the above details that the KNA contested mainly from KCM dominated ACs and remains mainly a party confining itself to the KCM group of people. It never won in any of the Naga dominated ACs.

National Peoples Party and the State Assembly Elections

It was as an attempt to build up a regional party with mass basis both in the mountains and plains but ultimately remained a party confining in the KCM dominated areas as it is obvious from the following details about its performance in the electoral politics of the State.

- 1990: Contested in five four in the valley on in the mountains which is a KC dominated AC and won only there (Lamlai, Uripok, Kumbi, Moirang, *Churachandpur*)

- 1995: Again contested in five, but this time no AC in the valley, all five in the mountains, three KCM dominated and two evenly poised ones, won in two KCM dominated ones (Chandel, Tamenglong, Saikot, *Churachandpur, Singhat*)

- 2000 in only one evenly poised AC, failed to win that one (Chandel)

- 2002: did not contest

- 2007: Contested in five ACs, three KCM dominated areas, one evenly poised and another in the valley, won in three, two KCM dominated and one evenly poised (*Thanlon, Singhat* Churachandpur, *Kangpokpi* and Konthoujam)

Manipur Hill Union

The Manipur Hill Union was a regional party which emerged after Statehood. During the 1974 elections, it put up 16 candidates, nine in Naga dominated ACs, five in KCM dominated ACs and another two in evenly poised ones. It won in seven Naga dominated, three KCM dominated and two evenly poised (Saitu, Karong, Saikul, Phungyar, *Chandel, Tengnoupal, Ukhrul, Chingai, Mao, Tadubi, Tamei, Tamenglong, Nungba, Thanlon, Churachandpur, Singhat*). This may be considered as sort of an exception in that it won both in Naga and Kuki-Chin-Mizo dominated areas and also in evenly contested areas. But then even this party contested no other subsequent elections and while it was there it remained more or less dominated by the Nagas. All these considerations point to the polarization of political parties on ethnic lines.

Polarization of electoral politics on ethnic lines has taken place not only in connections with political parties emerging from the mountains but also in time of the people casting their votes. This is obvious from the fact that nine of the Naga dominated ACs are usually won by the Nagas while the KCM dominated ACs are usually won by the KCM candidates while the remaining four remain keenly contested by the two. The polarization of voters on ethnic lines in time of electoral politics becomes all the more obvious from Tables 4.1 and 4.2 concerning the 15th Lok Sabha Elections, 2009.

Table 4.1
Maximum number of votes polled by two leading Naga and two leading Kuki-Chin-Mizo candidates in the nine Naga dominated ACs

Name of the nine Naga dominated constituencies	*No. of valid votes cast in favor of*				*No. of valid votes cast in favor of Kuki-Chin-Mizo candidates*	*No. of valid votes cast in favor of Naga candidates*
	1: Thangso Baite (INC)	*3: L.B. Sona (NCP)*	*2:D. Loli Adanee (BJP)*	*6: Mani Chare-namei (PDA)*		
43- Phungyar (ST)	3,523	22	4,199	12,523	3,545	16,722
44- Ukhrul (ST)	5,463	510	6,575	15,958	5,973	22,533
45- Chingai (ST)	3,374	303	5,021	22,194	3,677	27,215
47- Karong (ST)	9,984	25	12,281	17,443	10,009	29,724
48- Mao (ST)	850	21	23,317	21,330	871	44,647
49- Tadubi (ST)	4,935	67	13,295	16,481	5002	29,776
52- Tamei (ST)	5,905	46	2,526	18,815	5,951	21,341
53- Tamenglong (ST)	3,723	46	2,940	16,046	3,769	18,986
54- Nungba (ST)	9,050	72	3,470	4,770	9,122	8,240
Total	46,807	1,112	73,624	1,45,560	47,919	2,19,184

Table 4.2
Maximum number of votes polled by two leading Naga and two leading Kuki-Chin-Mizo candidates in the eight Kuki-Chin-Mizo dominated ACs

Name of the Kuki-Chin-Mizo dominated constituencies	*No. of valid votes cast in favor of*				*No. of valid votes cast in favor of Kuki-Chin-Mizo candidates*	*No. of valid votes cast in favor of Naga candidates*
	1: Thangso Baite (INC)	*2: L.B. Sona (NCP)*	*3:D. Loli Adanee (BJP)*	*4: Mani Chare-namei (PDA)*		
46- Saikul (ST)	27,516	273	1,100	3,610	27,789	4,710
51- Saitu (ST)	23,336	710	1,579	9,299	24,046	10,878
55- Tipaimukh (ST)	1,988	685	252	8,794	2,673	9,046
56- Thanlon (ST)	1,506	13,004	209	1,173	14,510	1,382
57- Henglep (ST)	19,829	1,911	509	1,124	21,740	1,633
58- Chura-chandpur (ST)	9,735	24,536	503	2,923	34,271	3,426
59- Saikot (ST)	30,290	3,826	720	3,178	34,116	3,898
60- Singhat (ST)	8,998	12,899	42	439	21,897	481
Total	1,23,198	57,844	4,914	30,540	1,81,042	35,454

2.e. Insurgency and continuing vulnerability of the Human Rights of the people

In Manipur, the late 1970s ushered in an era of armed conflict between the insurgents and the armed and uniformed personnel of the state. It witnessed the emergence of a number of insurgent organizations like the Peoples Revolutionary Party of Kangleipak (PREPAK - 1977), the Peoples Liberation Army (PLA-1998), etc. This was followed by the resurgence of the United National Liberation Front (UNLF-1964) since 1980 onwards. By September 8, 1980, the entire area of Manipur was declared a disturbed area. The very next day, i.e. September 9, 1980, saw the introduction of the Armed Forces Special Powers Act, 1958 (AFSPA) inside the State. This was again followed by the introduction of extraordinary laws like the Terrorist Activities Detention Act (TADA), 1985 (now repealed), National Security Act (NSA), 1980, the Punjab Security of the State Act, 1953, etc. At present, the problem of insurgency inside the State is far from waning. Indeed, it has become all the more serious with more and more armed groups emerging inside the State. There are at present not less than 30 militant groups inside the State. These can be again clearly divided into three groups – 1) those emerging from among the people living in the valley, 2) those emerging from among the Nagas, and 3) those emerging from among the Kuki-Chin-Mizo group of people. Certain basic incompatibilities in the aims and objectives of these groups render the problem all the more complex and complicated. While the Nagas insurgents stand for the unification of the Nagas inhabited areas into a single political unit (independent or otherwise), for the people in the valley, the mountains and plains of the State are two organic parts of Manipur and never to severe from one another. The Groups belonging to the Kuki-Chin-Mizo group of people also have not altogether given up their hopes to see a Kuki Zalengam (Kuki Homeland).

One of the immediate problems which followed the emergence of insurgency with renewed vigour since the late 1970s and the subsequent imposition of extraordinary laws has been that of the vulnerability of the human rights of the people. Soon, reports of violation of human rights of the people by the armed and uniformed personnel of the state started appearing in the local dailies with alarming frequency. These reports included alleged cases of arbitrary arrest, unlawful detention, disappearance of persons taken into custody, custodial deaths, rape by these personnel, killing of innocent people by them, victims of fake encounters, extreme physical and mental harassment of the people in the name of combing operations, unlawful invasion of people's privacy, etc. All these generated an unprecedented hue and cry against such human rights violations. This was accompanied by organized efforts on the part of the people to protect themselves from possible or actual violations of their human rights. It was against the backdrop of such an environmental context that *Meira Paibis* emerged in the valley of Manipur playing a most significant and visible role in the people's struggle for human rights inside the State. At present, the human rights interests of the people remain as vulnerable as ever and the struggle for the protection and promotion of the human rights still continues not only by women but also numerous civil society groups inside the State. The peoples' struggle for the protection and promotion of their human rights inside the State has been most significantly symbolized by Irom Chanu Sharmila Devi who has been on an indefinite fast since 2 November 2000 for the repeal of the notorious Armed Forces Special Powers Act.

2.f. State of Governance in Manipur

The term governance has become a very popular word nowadays in academic and public discussions. Basically governance means exertion of legal power and authority vested in the institutions and agencies of the government to carry out the avowed goals and purposes of the state. In this context, state has many goals or proposes for the realization of which it has come into existence. Some of the basic or primary aims of the state are to protect the rights and liberties of the people; to provide security life and property to them; etc. In other words, to secure to the people those conditions that will give them an opportunity to lead a better life. So governance would mean exertion of the legal power and authority vested in the institutions and agencies of the government with a view to achieve these things. Governance is also associated with efficient and effective administration in a democratic framework. It also involves exercise of political, economic and administrative powers of the state in managing affairs of the state. It also includes both the process of policy formulation and implementation. The concept of governance also has certain basic implications which may be listed as follows:

- People's human rights and fundamental freedoms have to be respected so that people within the state may lead a life of dignity.
- People should have a say in decisions that affect their lives.
- They also should be in a position to hold decision-makers accountable.
- Inclusive and fair rules, institutions and practices should govern social interactions.
- Women should be there as equal partners with men in private and public spheres of life and decision making.
- People should be free from discriminations based on caste, creed, ethnic, linguistic or gender considerations.
- The needs of the future generations should be reflected in the current policies.

- Economic and social policies should aim at eradicating poverty and expanding the choices that all people have in their lives.

Thus the question of governance has great relevance in the state democracy of a country. Because good governance is democratic governance, and there can be no democracy without good governance and vice versa. So it is important that there is good governance inside the State so that a truly democratic system prevails in Manipur. However, recurrent cries against violation of human rights of the people, threats to security of life and property, slow pace of economic development, worsening problem of drug abuse, corruption, unemployment, all too frequent bandhs, blockades, etc. tells a sorry state of governance inside the State.

2.g. Voting Behaviour in Manipur

Voting behaviour has emerged as an important concern for political scientists and researchers as it will play a significant role in making the electoral process of a country more meaningful. It shows whether the voters can exercise their voting rights meaningfully or not. The ability to do so on the part of the voters is a most important precondition for the success of democracy. The voters' intention to vote is a dynamic, changing and even fluid mental situation subject to influence and manipulation by many factors. Some of the important factors which influence voting behaviour of the people in general are ideology, personality of the candidates, party policies and programs, money, relationships, important socio political issues, economic conditions of the voters, their educational level, their groups identities and affiliations, etc.

Regarding the factors which influence the voting behaviour of the people of Manipur, some of the most important have been money, personal relationships, personality of the candidates, muscle power, important socio-political issues emerging from time to time, economic conditions of the voters, their educational level, their groups identities and affiliations, etc. By and large, the voters are not interested in ideologies. As such, the candidates begin to capitalize on kinship networks, close personal ties, etc. Where these things do not work, pre-election promises for personal and group benefits will be made. Then, as the day of polling comes knocking at the door, money will be used to win the voters. Finally, the use of muscle power will also be seen in the form of putting pressure on potential rivals not to contest elections, booth capturing, poll violence, manipulations of votes inside the polling station, threatening people not cast their votes or to cast their votes in favour of particular candidates, etc.

A general apathy towards manifestoes and policy and programs of the parties is also seen among the voters. This means they do not vote on the basis of the merit or otherwise of the parties. This is not surprising when we consider the fact that they are least interested in ideologies or policies or programs but in personalities, relationships, money, etc. Still there are some voters who are inclined to participate in a number of election related activities like that of election campaigns, election meetings, flag hoisting ceremonies, etc. They are enthusiastic about the voting, influencing other's vote, participating in political debates, wearing badges of political parties, distributing leaflets, etc. Even then, for the most of them also, once the election time is over, they tend to lose interest considerably in the political affairs of the State. All these mean that overall political participation of the people of the State is one of occasionally active level of participation rather than perennial interest in the issues of the land.

It may also be noted that there are voters who decide the person whom they will vote for well in advance but their number is again significantly less than those who decide the candidates only as the election closes in. Many also remain flaunting their undecided stand even after the actual voting process has started. This is an obvious baiting for money. Regarding the independent exercise of their votes, women are more influenced by their spouses than vice versa.

It may further be noted that the voters' interests in elections significantly differ depending on the level of elections. By and large they are more involved in local and State assembly elections than in Lok Sabha elections. The dissatisfaction of the voters with the performance of an outgoing government does not necessarily mean that they will vote it out. In other words, they are not so concerned with the performance of government while casting their votes. The voters of Manipur also have a tendency to cast for the party in power at the centre. This is in spite of the regional or local issues so vocally raised in time of election campaigns. In fact, though the people are more concerned with regional issues than national ones, on many occasions this has not been translated into the success of regional parties in the electoral politics of the State. It will be true in particular in the context of the last two State assembly elections. It is however, significant that by and large people believe in democracy as a form of government. They always prefer it to dictatorship.

5

The Manipuri Women and Changing World

—N. Vijaylakshmi Brara & Seromena Asem

The Key Issue: The Gender- Culture Debate

In many cultural and religious traditions, women have primary responsibility for transmitting cultural and spiritual knowledge and practices, as well as group identity, to succeeding generations. Because culture exists through, and is generated by, the lived experiences of people, the role of women in transmitting culture also situates them as creators and custodians of culture. For this reason, people across a diverse range of communities view women's adherence to and promulgation of cultural norms as integral to cultural survival. In many instances, this relationship between gender and culture is used as a basis for justifying violations of women's human rights. For example, in many cultures, religions, and states, the rights of individual women are subordinated to upholding women's role as the carriers of group identity. Thus, women are often denied the right to make autonomous decisions regarding their own sexuality, childbearing, and marriage; and their children's nationality, religion, and citizenship. These violations of basic rights are rationalized as necessary to ensure cultural preservation and other collective identities, which women are thought to embody.

On the other hand, women's primary role in transmitting and creating culture can serve as a basis for protecting and enhancing women's status within their families and communities. For example, the international indigenous women's movement has demonstrated that among many indigenous peoples, women's roles as spiritual guides, midwives, healers, and political leaders—all forms of cultural expression—are a central basis of women's power and status among their peoples. Indeed, women's cultural practices are important not only for the spiritual health of their communities, but also for their communities' overall well-being. In most communities around the world, women are the primary providers of food, water, and healthcare for their families. Women fulfil these roles in culturally specific ways, highlighting the relationship between women's gender-based human rights, cultural rights, and economic and social rights.

Women in Manipur too have been healers, spiritual guides, midwives as well as political leaders from time immemorial. The maibis, through their spirituality and their physical healing have been ensuring the well being of the whole society from ancient times. The *Meira-Paibis* on the other hand have provided the leadership in the political sphere, when no other group dared to transgress the arena of the conflict zones.

Women in Northeast India as a whole, just like their counterparts in South East Asia have been producers and seller from ancient times. They may not be big entrepreneurs but are economically self sufficient. Every household in the villages has a loom, a small or big kitchen garden and a *pukhari* (pond) with plenty of fishes. Traditionally women all over the North East weave. Their visibility is distinct as they themselves sell their produce in the markets. In Manipur these markets are called *Ima Keithel* (Mothers' markets). In Surakarta in Java islands **Klewer textile market is well known for the women vendors.** In fact all the traditional markets in Java Island are dominated by women. It is these very markets, their physical economic base, which also serves as their political intellectual base. The religious groupings in the form of the priestesses of the traditional religion, not only in Manipur but also in other parts of this region, have helped these women to acquire the strength which very few dare to challenge. The present women pressure groups derive this unchallengeable mundane (earthy) strength from this sacred tradition. Their strength lies in such collectives — socio-economic and religious.

There is this peculiar South East Asian trajectory which envelops the way we look at women collectives. In most of the south-east Asian societies, specially the Burmese, the Javanese and the Malaysian as well as in the North East India, the collective strength of women offers material self sufficiency and ensures a degree of co-operation with men in the social sphere. A woman's self-image in the North East, just like her counterparts in the Javanese and the Burmese societies generally speaking, is very much influenced by her role as a *mother,* which provides her a superior status and stable security compared to her wifely role. According to Dewi Candraningrum, "ordinary Javanese women are able to move quite freely outside of domestic life. Therefore, the miserable plights of widowhood as perceived in the other parts of India are absent here. Even in the realm of economy, the trade and commerce is traditionally handled by women in most of these societies.

Not so refreshing though, there are other similarities with the south-east and it is that we also share the common grounds of the conflict zone. Anybody with a little insight will tell that Burma's (Myanmar's) situation is very similar with that of the Northeast. Indonesia and Malaysia also had their fair share of political turmoil. Needless to say, that its impact on the women of this whole region is also similar. Their sufferings must be as heart rendering as ours.

The History of Motherhood

The assertive motherhood of the Manipuri women got manifested in the form of the two *nupilans* (women's fight) against the British. In 1903, the people revolting against the British rule burnt down the residence of the Assistant Superintendent. In 1904, Lt. Col. Maxwell, the political agent at that time ordered the people of Imphal to supply teak-wood from the Kabaw valley (now in Myanmar) and reconstruct the house. The women did not take it calmly, as in that order they read the re-introduction of the forced labour, which their king had earlier abolished. They entered the Residency and could not be controlled even by the military. The British were compelled to withdraw their order. **This *Nupilan* (an exclusive women's movement) also marked the first people's organized protest against the British.**

The women rose again in 1939 against the decision to export rice by the British in connivance with the local traders. This led to the acute shortage of the food-grain. Starvation was looming large. Women, who were already playing a significant role in the sphere of domestic trade and commerce, felt the gravity of the situation and once again *gheraoed* the British Residency to stop export of rice, "By early afternoon over a thousand women had assembled in the market, from whence they marched out to put pressure on Sharpe, the assistant to the Political Agent Mr. Grimson, to telegraph the Maharaja of Manipur, Sir Churachand (who was in Nabadwip, one of the holy places for the Hindus). The situation got improved at around 1.30 pm by the receipt of the telegram from the maharaja requesting the political agent to stop the export of rice with immediate effect. (Parrett, 2010: p115-119). A contingent of Assam Rifles had to be called in to rescue the British administrators. The protesting women were forcibly evicted, injuring scores of them and some were even pitched into the cold waters of the nearby ponds. This was the second *Nupilan*. In its memory Hijam Irabot, the communist leader of that time penned down the following lines:

Ngasi Ahing lelle/
Numit Ama chatkhre/
Sham Punsmountainu Devi/
Epha pharibado/
December 12 ama houkhre/
December 12 ama lakle/
(This night has passed/
A day has passed/
Devi, put your hair in a bun/
One December 12 has passed/
Another December 12 has come)

These lines penned by Hijam Irabot, the leader of Nikhil Manipur Mahasabha in his poem *'Imagi Puja* (worship of mothers) is repeatedly quoted by those who want to contribute a few lines with the coming of December in the memory of the bravery shown by the women of Manipur in *Nupilan* of 1939 on the 12th December which lasted for about a year. According to some scholars in Manipur; Hijam Irabot Singh with his anti-feudal agenda, was swift not only to jump on the bandwagon of the women's protest movement but also to seize its controls. In the MSA Record of Criminal Case 4, 1940: Manipur State vs. Hijam Irabot Singh, he said that, "we begged for rice and in turn received bayonet wounds, for one handful of rice we paid two handful of blood... Let us take revenge for the spilt blood of the *brahmini* (Brahmin woman).

The Women's work is finished and now has come the time for the men. (Parrett: 2010:129)

Interestingly, this protest which culminated as recognized women's movement resented the men who got involved at that stage. According to the reports of Gimson, "Men and boys were around the outside (of the protest), but when one of them interrupted a chat between me and one of them (women) she rounded on him and the men near him ran away":These women could not do much when a popular leader took over upon him and made the *Nupilan* of 1939 a prime agenda of his party. One needs to see, whether the 'taking over' of the issues from the women has led to the marginalization of their movement or has helped in metamorphosing into a bigger wave sustaining it in the long run. Nevertheless, the anti-colonial as well as the anti- feudal movements of that time, be it Indian National Congress or the *Nikhil Manipuri Mahasabha* of the Communists owe to the *Nupilan* of 1939 an incalculable debt. It was this women's war which generated political awareness in the masses and established the foundation for the aspiration for a just and egalitarian society. The ultimate victory of the women's struggle was that it managed to bring down the feudal regime and initiated the move to have democratic elections! These elections took place in 1948- four years before the first democratic elections in India. By November of that year the Maharaja was replaced by an elected Government. The tenure of this government was short lived as soon Manipur was merged with the new born concept called India.

Yet, the traditions set by the two Nupilan(s) live on. Mass women's protests by the Meira Paibis against the atrocities of the armed groups still goes on and after 53 years it has again made history. The naked protest of the women after the killing of Manorma has gone down in the history of Manipur as the third *Nupilan*.

Sir Robert Reid, the Governor of Assam in 1939 remarked that, 'Manipuri Women are notorious for their independence and their proneness to take direct action to get their own way'. He recalled that when a previous officiating political officer had attempted to introduce stricter regulations on the *Ima* markets, it resulted in his being surrounded by these women and threatened with a ducking in the river unless he withdrew certain orders'.

The Vigil groups

Manipuri women's groups are the vigil groups of their society. They are the Mothers. Like any other mother they can go to any extent to safeguard the lives and interests of their children— their society. Nowhere else, will one find such vast network of organizations of women. Their handling of the most difficult situations in most non-violent ways is remarkable. They are a treasure in themselves. Their organizational skills and their non-violent means, even in the face of barbaric violence can be a wonderful learning and sharing experience within the South Asian region.

In the present scenario we have strong women's front in every community in Manipur. Among the Meitei community (the valley based) it is the Meira-Paibies, the Naga Women's Union among the Nagas, the Kuki Women's Association, Lamkang Women's Union, Moyon Women's Union, Chothe Women's Union, the Tangkhul Shanao Long etc. among the various other mountain tribes. In short we have organized women's force in each tribe and community.

The ***"Meira Paibis"*** roam in the locality to keep a watch on drunkenness and drug-abuse. They are also protectors of the people against the repressive acts of the armed forces. They make a human wall in cases where innocent local youths are forcibly being taken away by the armed forces in the name of containing insurgents. They are the only ones who can dare to warn and scold the people in underground movement for their excesses. Everybody is cautious of them. They dare to get lathi charged, to sit for hunger strikes and even go to jail for a right cause.

So are the women's groups in the mountains. The Naga Mother's Association and the Kuki Women's Association and other women's groups of the various other tribes are the guardians of their respective tribe. They played a pivotal role during Naga-Kuki clashes, where barbarism of the worst kind got unleashed in its naked proportions in the name of ethnic cleansing. Even infants were beheaded. It was at that moment that NMA and KWA went hand in hand long stretches in the mountains (sometimes walking 3-4 days continuously) to meet their respective under-ground outfits to tell them to stop killing each other.

The major activity of these women's groups in the mountains include going from village to village preaching about peace and harmony, and conducting fasting programmes to end the ethnic clashes, and also to condemn, protest and demand compensation and judicial enquiry into killing of innocent villagers by the security forces. At the same time like the Meira-Paibies, they stand against the drug abuse, prostitution, alcoholism, gambling and the like vices affecting their society.

The women's associations are very strong and powerful bodies. But one also notices that empowerment of women however, is miserably inadequate considering the tremendous works done by them. The representation of women in Panchayat, Zilla Parishad etc. has not cut much ice as the women representations cannot come out of the corrupt political culture, thus diminishing their effectiveness in these institutions. There is a lone women MLA in the entire 60 member legislative assembly. In reverse to that we have very impressive representation of women in the lower rung of our democratic institutions. In fact we often cross the 33%

reservations granted to the women, where some women have been able to be elected from non-reserved seats. But, it has not changed the scenario. They are struggling to acquire their legitimate power from the patriarchal state machinery and even within the family.

Here in Manipur, the women did not have to strive to come out of boundaries of their homes. They have been socially visible outside the home front since a very long time. Moreover, they did not have to struggle to come out from the confines, in fact, certain traditions and also certain historical circumstances have brought our women in the forefront. It has also given them a unique status vis-à-vis their society. I can also say at the outset that here one gets instances where many elements in the feminist pāradigms falters while many observations enlighten us with new aspects in gender relations. But, as said earlier, even though one may presume the status of Manipuri women to be high, it has to be critically examined and analyzed from an insiders' perspective.

The collective strength of the Meira Paibis reminds me of *Anarchist feminism* which is a theory that female subordination is determined as much by a system of sexual and familial relationships as by State controls, and that legal change cannot in itself provide equality without full psychological autonomy. Anarchist feminism would eliminate all social restraints and replace these with decentralized, organic communities of women. Anarchist feminists argue that the State and patriarchy are twin irregularities. To obliterate the State is to destroy the major instrument of institutionalized patriarchy; to abolish patriarchy is to put an end to the State.

This theory is more avant-garde than radical feminism because it believes that any State is always illicit. Anarchist feminists also believe that the means used to revolutionize the society must be the models of the future society in themselves. Therefore, women's cooperatives and consciousness-raising groups can make a more momentous social and ideological input than their numbers or financial status might entail. *Anarchist feminism* refers to the inspiration feminists have gained from the concept of anarchy from the Greek word, literally, non-rule.

The foremother of anarchist feminism, Emma Goldman (1869-1940), opined that political ideas were meaningless unless they were acted on, and she was arrested numerous times for speaking out and advocating such action. As a nihilist, she knew that men and women are oppressed by authoritarian social structures, but she also saw that women are oppressed specifically as women. The convergence of feminist concerns with anarchism meant that no mere reform of hierarchical institutions would be adequate to the task of allowing women to live full lives. Thus, she spoke out against women's suffrage because she saw it as merely a way to gain women's cooperation in the maintenance of an essentially unchanged organization.

The backgrounds against which the Meira Paibis are working are the protests against the state laws and their oppressions. They are, in other words fighting against the State and its patriarchal edifice and therefore can be called anarchist feminists, but on the societal patriarchal fronts they do not seem to feel the need to challenge the norms and traditions as they fall coterminous to their identity and their notions of their nation.

There is a very interesting argument mooted in defence of the customs and traditions of our society as a whole and it is that we are far better of than our counterparts in the mainland India where women are not even allowed to be born, where female infanticide and bride burning is a regular feature. On top of it our women are very visible. As mentioned above, we have women's organizations in every community.

They are very visible. They are sitting in protests and carrying on peace efforts. But, where are their voices in the decision-making bodies? There is an unwritten dictum telling them that you can go so far and no more. This attempt to shut them down with attempts to compare degrees of oppression entails further problems. The subtle codes in the garb of rigid social norms extending to the political sphere, denying them to live their lives with dignity are more difficult to handle than the stark and bold discriminatory practices in other parts of India.

First and foremost, gender has to become an issue.

Here we need to discuss the issues relating to polygamy, domestic violence and other forms of division of labour. Discussion on reforming the customary laws has to be initiated. The process of gender sensitization of the whole state machinery is another pertinent issue. The questions of development, illiteracy, and health problems should be discussed. We will also have to ponder as to how much physical as well as mental space have been given to our women. Involving the women in the decision-making process and institutions should be our goal.

Women and Peace

Whenever there is violation of 'Peace' in society, it is seen that its first impact is always felt by women and therefore in negotiating for peace women must play a decisive role.

A number of international commitments outline women's right to full involvement in political and economic decision-making, including numerous resolutions of the General Assembly and the Economic and Social Council, the Convention on the Elimination of All Forms of Discrimination Against Women (CEDAW), the 1995 Beijing Platform for Action and United Nations Security Council resolution 1325 (2000) on women and peace and security.

In one of the statements made by the Beijing Platform for Action, in a world of continuing instability and violence, the implementation of cooperative approaches to peace and security is urgently needed. The equal access and full participation of women in power structures and their full involvement in all efforts for the prevention and resolution of conflicts are essential for the maintenance and promotion of peace and security. Although women have begun to play an important role in conflict resolution, peace keeping and defence and foreign affairs mechanism, they are still underrepresented in decision-making positions. If women are to play an important part in securing and maintenance of peace, they must be empowered politically and economically and represented adequately at all levels of decision making."

Implementing these commitments would be a first step toward utilizing all available resources to establish and sustain peace. When approaching the difficult task of ending conflict, the stakes are too high to neglect the resources that women have to offer. Examples from around the world illustrate their contributions.

Why Involve Women?

UNIFEM , in one of its documents has cited the need and importance of involving women in peace negotiations validating through the experiences from all over the world over. According to their observation:

Women's organizations persistently advocate for peace. Their focus and demand can be instrumental in initiating formal peace negotiations, maintaining support for the process and facilitating implementation of the accords. In Colombia, for example, despite repeated attacks, disappearances, kidnappings and threats against women leaders, they continue to organize, develop agendas for peace and lobby for their implementation.

Women often build a foundation for peace negotiations. In Northern Ireland, for example, women's groups spent a decade building trust between Protestants and Roman Catholics, creating a foundation upon which the agreements would ultimately be built. By highlighting the personal cost of the violence and drawing attention to the tangible effects of war on people's lives, they convinced both the parties to the negotiations and the public that "living and the quality of life...were the issues that mattered"—even more than the contentious political issues being negotiated.

Women can catalyze pcace negotiations. In Sri Lanka, a leading businesswoman began a massive awareness-raising campaign to support the start of negotiations in 2001. More than one million Sri Lankans publicly demonstrated their support for peace, pressuring leaders to begin peace talks.

Women can build ties among opposing factions. In Somalia, women presented themselves as a "sixth clan" at the National Reconciliation Conference in Arta, Djibouti, reaching beyond clan divisions to a "vision of gender equality." They ultimately assisted in the creation of a National

Charter that guaranteed women 25 seats in the 245-member Transitional National Assembly.

Women can increase the inclusiveness, transparency and sustainability of the peace process. During South Africa's post-apartheid transition, a coalition of women's groups advocated for and achieved a more democratic process for constitutional and legislative reform. A participatory approach that required the government to seek civil society input on proposed policies was adopted. This resulted in the expansion of the definition and scope of security and allowed the population to articulate its concerns in a national dialogue on security sector reform.

Women can bring a different perspective from men to negotiations, raising issues that might otherwise be ignored. In El Salvador, women leaders at the negotiation table and in implementation committees ensured that the names of women fighters, as well as non-combatant supporters of the opposition movement, were included in beneficiary lists for land and other resources. Providing for supporters, in particular, averted a near certain crisis among the peasant population and was something their male colleagues had neglected up to that point.

A gender perspective in the peace process can lead to long-term advances for women's equality. Among the 500 representatives to Afghanistan's Congressional drafting committee, 102 were women of various languages, ethnicities and political affiliations. Overcoming many obstacles, their presence and persistence led to a guarantee of women's equality in the final draft of the new constitution, including a quota for women in the lower house of parliament.

Women can foster reconciliation and provide an example for moving society forward. In Rwanda, women formed the first cross-party parliamentary caucus, composed of both Hutus and Tutsis, addressing issues of concern to women from all political parties. This set the precedent for other cross-party caucuses to be established.

Women often work to sustain the peace agreement at all levels. In Bougainville in 1998, women returned from peace talks to their communities and were reportedly the only leaders to initiate an information campaign for the public to comprehend the decisions of the peace accord and the next steps in its implementation.

Way Forward: How can the involvement of women in peace negotiations be effective?

Ensuring women's effective participation involves a range of actions. Even before peace processes officially begin, the state machinery can support diverse women's peace-building activities at local and national levels, facilitating their development of a common agenda for peace, and strengthening their capacity as leaders to prepare them for the negotiating table and the post-conflict transition.

During the negotiations, women from various backgrounds and ethnicities must be brought forward in official and informal capacities so that the voices and experiences of women throughout the state will be considered during decision-making that will affect all of society. And once the agreement is signed, women must continue to participate in implementation and monitoring mechanisms, ensuring that the priorities of half the population are allocated resources and attention in the post-conflict environment.

Ultimately, the peace process is compromised when women do not participate. It has been recognized that inclusiveness is necessary to ensure the legitimacy of the decision-making process, to encourage a broad base of participation and to make sustainable peace and development possible.

Given the difficulties inherent in negotiating peace, attempts to bring women's voices to the talks are most successful when those voices are unified in their demands. However, like men, women differ dramatically in their political ideas, affiliations and attitudes, making them anything but a homogenous group. Their perspectives hinge on their experiences during the conflict, which will vary according to race, ethnicity, religion, class, age, profession and geographic location, among other factors. Thus when women are able to formulate a consensus-based platform, their diversity adds tremendous credibility, legitimacy and force to their demands. Supporting women from diverse regions and backgrounds to unite around common priorities for peace and reconstruction—in order to inform negotiations— can be a first step to increasing women's effective involvement in the peace process.

Throughout this process, it is critical to have governmental and civil society support to be advisory and facilitative, rather than prescriptive, so that local women's groups can take full ownership of any final decisions taken, recommendations drafted or networks created.

A variety of exercises have proven useful to facilitate a common platform. First, a diverse group of recognized women leaders must be chosen from among relevant constituencies. Thus—often as a result of the diversity of the group—significant time is necessary to allow the women to meet and begin to trust one another, particularly as they may be coming from opposing sides of a conflict.

Women leaders often recognize that a strategic alliance between women's groups can be based on a minimum common agenda of securing women's place at the peace table, allowing them to set aside other differences temporarily. At this early stage, capacity-building and technical training on mediation and negotiations are also critical in order to prepare women to participate in the official process, honing their abilities and maximizing their contribution.

Women and Economy

According to the United Nations Organisation, 70 per cent of the 1.3 billion people who live in absolute poverty around the globe are women. Majority of women in developing countries carry the enormous burden of poverty and discrimination. Living under poverty implies poor nutrition, high illiteracy, children not enrolled in schools, high infant and maternal mortality, inadequate health care, no access to good drinking water, poor sanitation, lack of proper shelter and extreme vulnerability to shocks associated with natural and human events resulting in debt bondage and further deprivation. Further, it is marked by a condition of both assetlessness and powerlessness.

In Economics, the concept of human capital defines people as capital assets. And the quality of human resource/capital has an important influence on the process of economic growth. Such assets are formed by long-term and sustained investments in humans, i.e., through investments in 'education' and 'health-care services'. While education helps to improve one's mental capability and imparts skills, health-care services help improve the physical capability. It is logical to say that educated and healthy people, by and large, are capable of making better choices in any life situation. They are innovative and have greater degree of geographical and social mobility. Therefore, if a large section of human beings, the women, remains in ill-health, illiterate and in limited freedom etc., then the process of growth is constrained. Rather, this segment of population becomes a constraint to growth. In other words, real development cannot take place without involving women. As the World Development Report, 2004 puts it, "education contributes to better health, and better education and health increase the productivity that lead to economic growth. Growth then generates resources that finance improvements in people's health and education, further raising productivity. Gender equality is central in these synergies because women are the agents of development".

Three guiding principles are now accepted as important considerations in social policy making and societal development. They are *gender equity, resource ethics and empowerment of women.* Equality, empowerment and sustainability of natural resources are broad terms that have links with almost every initiative for improving women status. Gender equity or equality implies a society in which women and men enjoy the same opportunities, outcomes, rights and obligations in all spheres of life.

Empowerment of women is the enhancement of the capability and sphere of action for women, with a focus on identifying and redressing power imbalances and giving women more autonomy to manage their own lives. This can be achieved through enhancing economic participation, educational attainment, health and survival levels and political participation. The relative importance of these different dimensions would depend upon the social, cultural and development level of the society.

Global development so far has depended heavily on the exploitation of natural resources, leading to not only the depletion of the resources themselves but to the presently universal worry of global warming. This has affected the lives of women even more adversely than those of men. All these have necessitated the humankind to examine the relative priority of present and future generations in the use of natural resources, and also the relative effects of resource use on the two sexes. It is now accepted that future generations should left with the same level of resources as being enjoyed by the present generation.

Now let us examine the scenario of Manipur in all the different dimensions of the position of women.

The Case of Manipur

Manipur is a predominantly rural, tradition bound and culturally diverse region inhabited by a heterogeneous population. People are dependent mainly on primary sector activities based on land, forests, and livestock, with construction emerging as the main activity in recent years. The province is divided into nine districts: four valley districts and five mountain districts. These geographically contiguous districts share historical roots that are intertwined and socio-cultural similarities, especially the patriarchal domination. The natural beauty, rich cultural heritage and the economic engagement of women of this land are widely appreciated. As regards women, contemporary scholars even go to the extent of characterising Manipuri women as holding up half the sky.

A thorough study of the Manipuri history from the ancient time reveals that women in our Manipur have played a very significant role in various periods. The mythical Laisana, queen of the First King of Manipur, Nongda Lairen Pakhangba, was the President of the Patcha. Patcha was a special women's court where all women related cases were taken up and settled. Queen Linthoingambi is still remembered for her presence of mind and courage while dealing with the Tangkhul tribes during the absence of the King Ningthoukhomba (1432-1467). There is also a long list of many historically acclaimed political uprisings of women, the 1904 and 1939 events who are even today, a continuous source of inspiration to the Manipuris. We can safely vouch that women of Manipur still retain their character and role. It is as if time has not changed this. Women of Manipur still today continue to play a leading and critical role in spearheading mass movements for realization of social goals. One active manifestation of women's involvement in the economic sphere is the Khwairamband Keithel, generally known as the Ima Keithel. Here women are display preservation and maintenance of the peculiar elements and ideologies identifying the own culture and traditions of Manipur. Being impressed by this participation in socio-economic sphere, T.C. Hodson in his highly referred book, "*The Meitheis*" opined that "The Women hold a high and free position in Manipur, all the internal trade and exchange of the produce of the country being managed by them".

We can now look at social, political and economic status of the women in Manipur by examining the four fundamental indicators. We have taken:

- Social indicators
- Economic indicators
- Political indicators
- Health and Survival indicators.

Social indicators

In social indicators, we shall focus on education. In this

we shall examine three variables- educational attainments, literacy rate and educational outcomes in terms of attained levels.

Education: Literacy and education define the progress of individuals and their levels of understanding in dealing with day-to-day activities. Literacy is the primary condition for an individual who is able to read and write, while education is the level where the body and mind have been strengthened by the power of better understanding. Literacy is an important indicator of the relative development of a society and has a strong impact on the individuals' earnings leading to higher income and a more equal distribution of such income. Education is also considered as an important factor which could shape up not only the personality of an individual but could also develop the social setup of the community as a whole. Improving the educational status of female in itself, and vis-à-vis that of male, has been accepted as an important input for enhancing the quality of any social setup. That is why education is considered to be the best instrument of human resource development.

Table 5.1

Proportion of Female in Total Enrolment, 1990-2001

Year	*Per centage of Female in Total Enrolment in Primary School*	*Per centage of Female in Total Enrolment in Middle School*	*Per centage of Female in Total Enrolment in High/ Higher Secondary*	*Per centage of Female in Total Enrolment in Graduates and above*
1990-1991	45.3	46.4	44.8	42.8
1995-1996	48.2	44.7	45.8	41.3
2000-2001	48.8	47	46.6	47.2

Source: *Statistical Abstract Manipur, 2005,* Directorate of Economics and Statistics, Government of Manipur.

Enrolment in Educational Institutions: Enrolment is an important indicator of the relative access to educational facilities. In the absence of more recent data, we provide in Table 5.1 a picture of enrolment scenario during the decade 1990-91 to 2000-01. The general picture emerging is one where the proportion of women in the total enrolment is moving towards absolute parity with that of men though very slowly. The scenario is not however one of great disappointment.

Literacy rate: The trend of the relative literacy rate of the two sexes is shown in Table 5.2.

Table 5.2

Trends of Male and Female Literacy Rate in Manipur, 1901-2011

Year of Census	*Male*	*Female*	*Gender differential*
1901	1.86	0.04	1.82
1911	4.04	0.12	3.92
1921	7.65	0.15	7.50
1931	6.40	0.30	6.1
1941	9.77	0.61	9.16
1951	20.77	2.38	20.4
1961	45.12	15.93	35.75
1971	46.04	19.53	30.83
1981	53.29	29.06	27.66
1991	71.63	47.60	24.03
2001	80.30	60.60	19.7
2011	86.49	73.17	13.32

Source: A. *Census of India.*

B. *Economic Survey Manipur, 2002-2003*, Directorate of Economic and Statistics, Government of Manipur.

Note: Though no specific criterion was provided, the population was divided into two classes of literate and illiterate in the 1901 Census. In the subsequent censuses of 1911, 1921 and 1931, literacy was defined as the ability to write a letter and read the response. In the Censuses of 1951, 1961 and 1971 literacy rate is estimated on the basis of population aged 5 years and above while the population aged 7 years and above is accounted in the Censuses of 1981, 1991, 2001 and 2011.

Modern education for women in Manipur started lately in 1899-90 and got its momentum only after the British administration of Manipur. The Primary school for girls was opened in December 1899 with 12 pupils and this number increased to 53 at the end of the year. Female literacy rate was quite low that it did not even touch 1 percentage point during the colonial period. This could be due primarily to (i) the unimportance attached to female education then; (ii) the reluctance of the females themselves to attend schools for western education, which was then considered to be impure; iii) the requirement for older girls to stay at home to take care of siblings when mothers are away at work; iv) lack of relevance of school curriculum; and v) need for girls to work in order to help in augmenting the family income. With the phenomenal expansion of the formal education system since 1950 there has been a noticeable progress both for male and female literacy rates, but there is an undesirable continuance of gender disparity. The period between 1951 and 1961 stands out as the landmark in the history of literacy movement in Manipur. During this period the literacy rate underwent a quantum jump for both the sexes. No period after this has had such a phenomenon expansion in literacy rate. Both male and female literacy rate have been rising continuously after colonial period with 1951-61 as the landmark decade. Though there still persists gender disparity in literacy rates, an element of female literacy catching up fast is visible.

Attained Levels: Educational attainment is, no doubt, the most fundamental prerequisite for empowering women in all spheres of society, for without education of comparable quality and content to that given to boys and men, and relevant to existing knowledge and real needs, women are unable to access well-paid, formal sector jobs, advance within them, participate in, and be represented in government and gain political influence.

A picture of the outcome of education provision measured in terms of levels attained is shown in Table 5.3. Here the relatively more robust placing of women in Manipur as compared to the national average is visible in terms of both the negative indicator of Not Literate and the rest positive indicators. This does not, however, imply the prevalence of equity in educational attainment between the two sexes in Manipur. Whereas the proportion of female literates up to the primary level is higher than that of male, it goes down much below the proportion of the male in all the other indicators of educational attainment.

Economic indicators

It is generally held that economic growth brings about enhancements in the quality of life as well as improvements in the interpersonal relationships. The increasing employment of women outside the household, which generally accompanies economic development, is also believed to serve these ameliorative purposes to a great extent.

Employment, which is considered to be one of the major tools for empowerment of women, helps to empower people socially, economically and politically. It empowers people economically by giving them purchasing power of goods and services, socially by offering a productive role that enhances their dignity and self-esteem, and politically if they begin to influence decision-making in the workplace and beyond.

Simone de Beauvoir, a pioneer of modern feminism[1], wrote in her 1949 book *The Second Sex* thus: "It is through gainful employment that women have traversed most of the distance

Table 5.3
Per 1000 Distribution of Persons of 15 years and above by General Educational Level, 2004-05

States/All India	*not-literate*		*literate & up to primary*		*middle*		*Secondary*		*higher secondary*		*diploma/ certificate*		*graduate & above*	
	F	*M*	*F*	*M*	*F*	*M*	*F*	*M*	*F*	*M*	*F*	*M*	*F*	*M*
(1)	*(2)*	*(3)*	*(4)*	*(5)*	*(6)*	*(7)*	*(8)*	*(9)*	*(10)*	*(11)*	*(12)*	*(13)*	*(14)*	*(15)*
Arunachal Pradesh	493	336	219	260	136	151	84	99	44	81	4	9	18	64
Assam	340	173	352	372	179	237	71	109	40	61	0	4	16	43
Manipur	310	134	235	209	204	259	121	182	64	102	6	12	55	97
Meghalaya	170	131	513	492	167	218	69	67	34	43	4	9	42	36
Mizoram	33	14	411	320	343	372	122	166	58	60	3	5	27	61
Nagaland	216	128	216	170	263	282	133	139	116	148	4	14	52	119
Sikkim	320	165	378	469	133	164	97	104	48	50	2	2	21	46
Tripura	295	155	397	391	180	250	72	102	26	51	1	3	28	48
All-India	504	264	199	256	128	192	78	125	44	72	8	17	40	73

Source: NSSO, (2006), *Status of Education and Vocational Training: NSS 61st Round (July 2004-June 2005)*, Government of India.

that separated her from the male; nothing else can guarantee her liberty in practice". Frederick Engels also stated in *The Origin of the Family, Private Property and the State* that the "emancipation of women can only be possible when women can take part in production on a large social scale, and domestic work no longer claims anything but an insignificant amount of her time".

> **Simone de Beauvoir (January 9, 1908 – April 14, 1986) was a French existentialist (philosopher and writer. Her most famous and influential philosophical work *The Second Sex (1949)* is generally regarded as fundamental** to the development **of the women's movement** of the 1960s as well as **to the discipline of feminist studies.** After the **publication of this classic,** Beauvoir became widely **known and was hailed as** "the mother of second wave **feminism". Her other works** include *She Came to Stay (1943), **Memoirs of a Dutiful** Daughter (1958),* and ***All Men are Mortal (1946).***

From this perspective, we can now see the sex-wise scenario of a) working and non-working population; b) the occupational structure; and d) wage differentials in Manipur.

Workers and Non-Workers Population of the State by Sex

In India, the population between the ages 15 and 59 are usually divided into three categories according to the type of work they perform. They are Main workers, Marginal workers and Non-workers. Main workers are those persons engaged in economically productive activity for more than half the year, i.e., 183 days or more. Marginal workers refer to the persons engaged in economically productive work for less than 183 days in a year. Non-workers are those not engaged in any productive work at all during the year.

Table 5.4
Working and Non-working Population in Manipur, 1981-2001 (As percentage of the relevant total male and female in worker categories of the State)

Year	*Main Workers*		*Marginal Workers*		*Non-Workers*	
	Male	*Female*	*Male*	*Female*	*Male*	*Female*
1981	**45.9**	**34.6**	**0.9**	**4.9**	**53.2**	**60.5**
1991	**44.2**	**32.7**	**1.7**	**6.3**	**54.7**	**61.1**
2001	**39.3**	**21.4**	**8.9**	**17.6**	**51.9**	**60.9**

Source: Census of India **as reproduced in** ***Statistical Abstract Manipur, 2005,*** **Directorate of Economics and Statistics, Government of Manipur.**

In Table 5.4 we see a broad picture of the employment scenario during the twenty year period from 1981 to 2001, the period for which we have confirmed census figures. It is seen from the table a worsening scenario in this aspect for both the sexes as evident from the rise in the proportion of Marginal Workers accompanied by a fall in that of Main Workers. But this has affected the female worse than the male as seen from the rise in the gap in proportion of Main Workers between the sexes while at the same time the female proportion of Marginal Workers has risen sharper than that of male.

Economic Classification of Main Workers, 1961-2001

We can have a picture of the intra sex-wise distribution of Main Workers for the period from 1961-2001. In Table 5.5, this picture is given in terms of the three traditional divisions of activities into Primary, Secondary and Tertiary.

One very prominent picture emerging from Table 5.5 is the element of confirmation of the general perception of economy of Manipur being sustained by the womenfolk. This is borne out by two scenarios emerging from the table. First, there is the greater proportion of women being engaged in the primary sector as compared to that of male. Second, there is now the trend of women diversifying into newer areas in the tertiary sector at the rate faster than that of male.

Table 5.5

Distribution of Main Workers of Manipur by Main Industrial Categories and Sex, 1961-2001 (in per centages)

Industrial	***1961***		*1971*		*1981*		*1991*		*2001*	
Category	***Male***	***Female***	*Male*	*Female*	*Male*	*Female*	*Male*	*Female*	*Male*	*Female*
1	*2*	*3*	*4*	*5*	*6*	*7*	*8*	*9*	*10*	*11*
					Primary sectors					
Cultivators	**77.1**	**53.2**	**68.06**	64.93	63.96	63.09	**58.65**	66.18	40.65	48.42
Agricultural Labourers	**0.65**	**0.57**	3.53	3.88	3.31	7.29	4.62	9.6	5.90	7.17
Fishing, Hunting, Livestock Plantation, Orchard & allied activities	**0.31**	**0.13**	**0.83**	0.22	1.45	0.31	**2.09**	0.69	-	-
Mining & Quarrying	-	-	**0.03**	0.01	0.04	0.03	**0.04**	0.02	-	-
Sub Total	**78.06**	**53.90**	72.45	69.04	68.76	70.72	**65.40**	76.49	46.55	55.59
					Secondary Sectors					
Manufacturing,	3.98	41.12	2.4	22.91	2.01	20.17	1.45	11.95	3.33	12.58

(Contd...)

1	2	3	4	5	6	7	8	9	10	11
Processing, Servicing & Repairs										
a) Household Industry										
b) Other than Household Industry	0.46	0.15	1.86	1.23	2.36	1.02	2.72	1.74	-	-
Construction	1.09	0.13	1.85	0.07	3.05	0.28	2.37	0.38	-	-
Sub Total	5.53	41.4	6.11	24.21	7.42	21.47	6.54	14.07	3.33	12.58
Tertiary Sectors										
Trade & Commerce	2.90	3.75	3.12	4.37	3.14	3.7	4.18	3.35	-	-
Transport, Storage and Communication	1.64	0.01	1.63	0.04	1.53	0.03	1.97	0.12	-	-

(Contd...)

1	2	3	4	5	6	7	8	9	10	11
Other Services	11.85	0.92	16.69	2.33	19.15	4.06	21.91	5.97	50.05	31.83
Sub Total	16.39	4.68	21.44	6.74	23.82	7.79	28.06	9.44	50.05	31.83
Total	100	100	100	100	100	100	100	100	100	100

Source: Census Publications of the Office of the Registrar General, India.

Note: 1. Figures shown in the category *Other Services* in the year 2001 refers to other workers i.e., those engaged in some economic activity during the last one year, but not as cultivators or agricultural labourers or manufacturing, processing, servicing and repairing in household industry.
2. Figures for 2001 exclude Mao-Maram, Paomata and Purul Sub-Division of Senapati District.

Wage Differentials

One indicator of labour market discrimination is the gender gap in wages. This gap, if any, has implications for social justice and gender equality. We examine this scenario in Table 5.6.

Whereas it was seen earlier that women have been catching up with male in every sphere of modern employment, the scenario prevailing in the gender gap in wages is not favourable to women. In this the rural scenario, with average female wage being only about 53 per cent of the male wage, is far worse than the urban scenario where the average female wage constitutes about 81 per cent. Further, the rural scenario in Manipur is worse than that of India as a whole.

In the Northeast, the scenario in this regard is best in Mizoram and Sikkim.

Table 5.6
Average Wage[1]/ Salary[2] Earnings (Rs. 0.00) per day Received by Regular Wage/ Salaried Employees of Age 15-59 years

State	*Rural*			*Urban*		
	Male	*Female*	*Female Wage as Per centage of Male Wage*	*Male*	*Female*	*Female Wage as Per centage of Male Wage*
Assam	145.51	73.83	50.74	249.81	151.31	60.57
Bihar	175.97	96.72	54.96	249.61	209.45	83.91
Manipur	215.82	114.34	52.98	266.74	216.94	81.33
Meghalaya	194.21	158.75	81.74	288.69	213.57	73.98
Mizoram	280.38	291.07	103.83	292.10	319.36	109.33
Nagaland	279.79	211.61	75.63	275.28	223.12	81.05
Sikkim	203.43	207.31	101.91	233.39	224.79	96.31
Tripura	136.03	86.36	63.49	177.04	120.13	67.85
All-India	144.93	85.53	59.01	203.28	153.19	75.36

Source: NSSO, (2006), *Employment and Unemployment Situation in India, 2004-05, (Part – I):* 61st Round, Government of India.

Health and Survival Indicators

Development is conceptualized amongst other as widening the choices of the people. In this the level of education and general health of the population play an important role in not only achieving development but also as an important outcome of the development process. In fact, good health is both means and ends of development. In a Declaration adopted by the world community in 1978, and reflected in the Alma Ata declaration of the World Health Organization (WHO), health is classified as a human right. The 'health' of a person or of a group of people is a comprehensive concept that incorporates many dimensions, not just the absence of illness. In fact, the Charter of the World Health Organization (WHO) explicitly defines 'health' as 'a state of complete physical, mental and social well-being and not merely the absence of disease and infirmity'. This is the definition that recognizes the many dimensions of health and well-being, and one that requires action on many different fronts. India continues to occupy the lowest rung in comparison to the world's average health and survival indicators. India ranks 132nd position in the health and survival sub index among the 134 countries in the world as of 2010.

Given the discouraging scenario of India, it would be both necessary and rewarding to see the picture of Manipur in relation to the longevity and other health and survival indicators in order to examine the inter-sex differences in these indicators.

Sex Ratio

Let us start with the picture of number of Female per 1000 Male (sex ratio). This is an important demographic indicator in which a closer balance between the sexes is globally accepted as a healthy sign of population situations. It also indirectly indicates the status of women in a society.

We must say that the picture of Manipur has not been bad overall insofar as sex ratio is concerned. Right from the 1881 census till the 1961census, the ratio has been in favour of female. As seen from Table 5.7, the ratio started being unfavourable in 1971 census and the trend continued till the 1991 census. But from the 2001 census we observe signs of recovery.

Table 5.7

Sex Ratio of Manipur, 1881-2011

Year	*Females per thousand males*
1881	1,018
1901	1,037
1911	1,029
1921	1,041
1931	1,065
1941	1,055
1951	1,036
1961	1,015
1971	980
1981	971
1991	958
2001	974
2011	987

Source: A. *Census Publication of the Office of the Registrar General,* India.
B. NEC, *Basic Statistics of the North Eastern Region 2002,* Smountainong, 2004.

Life expectancy at Birth

Life Expectancy at Birth (LEB) is defined as the number of years a person may be expected to live when born, given the prevailing mortality rates of the population of the region. It gives us an idea of the longevity of a person given the health care facilities available in the region. The life expectancy data for Manipur are available only for the year 1991. The LEB for Manipur is lower than the national average. Within the State it is higher for women in both rural and urban areas. In rural areas it stands at 60.40 years for female and 56.70 years for male, and the urban figure stands respectively at 62.30 and 60.60 years. For the State as a whole, the female figure is 61.50 years as compared to 58.00 years for male. The possible explanation for this difference could be food habits and biological.

Infant Mortality Rate

The infant mortality rate is defined as the probability of a child dying before attaining the age of one year, and is calculated per 1000 live births. It is an important indicator reflecting a country's level of socio-economic development and quality of life, and is also used for monitoring and evaluating population and health programmes and policies. Manipur has one of the best (lowest) infant mortality rates in the country, nest only to Goa. But within the State, the rate has been moving in favour of male as compare to that of female. The respective rates for male and female were 18 and 13 in 2003, but in 2008 these stood at 13 and 15 respectively.

Maternal Mortality Rate

The maternal mortality rate refers to the number of deaths from child birth related causes occurring among the female population of a given geographical area during a given year, per 1,00,000 live births occurring among the population of the given geographical area during the same year. The significance of this indicator lies amongst others in its close relationship with the quality of and access to health care facilities in the region. Unlike the infant mortality rate, Manipur wears a sorry picture in this indicator; the rate in Manipur stands at 374 (2003) as compared to the national average of 301 (2005). This could be because of the lack of access to healthcare facilities in child-birth (Table 5.8).

Maternal Care

Health and well-being is a concept related to the substantial differences between women and men in their access to sufficient nutrition, healthcare and reproductive facilities, and to issues of fundamental safety and integrity of person. According to the World Health Organization, 585,000 women die every year, over 1,600 every day, from causes related to pregnancy and childbirth.

Table 5.8

Maternal Care Indicators, Manipur and All-India

State/All India	*Percentage of births delivered in a health facility*	*Percentage of deliveries assisted by health personnel**
Manipur	45.9	59.0
India	38.7	46.6
Mizoram	59.8	65.4

Source: *National Family Health Survey (NFHS-3), 2005-06,* India, IIPS, Volume I, p.220.

**Note:* Doctor, Auxiliary nurse mid-wife, nurse, midwife, lady health visitor, or other health personnel.

Food Consumption

As regards food consumption, the scenario is not unfavourable to women as evident from Table 5.9.

Prevalence of Anaemia

Three levels of severity of anaemia are distinguished: mild anaemia (10.0-10.9 grams/decilitre for pregnant women, 10.0-11.9 g/dl for non-pregnant women, and 12.0-12.9 g/dl for men), moderate anaemia (7.0-9.9 g/dl for women and 9.0-11.9 g/dl for men), and severe anaemia (less than 7.0 g/dl for women and less than 9.0 g/dl for men). Here the picture in

Table 5.9

Women's Food Consumption by State and All India, 2005-06

(Percentage of Women and Men Age 15-49 Consuming Specific Foods At Least Once A Week)

State/All India	*Milk or curd*		*Pulses or Beans*		*Dark green leafy vegetables*		*Fruits*		*Eggs*		*Fish*		*Chicken or Meat*		*Fish/ Chicken/ Meat*	
	M	*F*	*M*	*F*	*M*	*F*	*M*	*F*	*M*	*F*	*M*	*F*	*M*	*F*	*M*	*F*
Manipur	36.2	28.3	84.2	77.0	96.6	97.0	67.5	68.6	44.0	37.3	63.3	65	40.2	18	72.0	70.7
India	67.2	55.4	90.7	89.5	93.6	92.9	47.4	39.8	41.3	32.3	31.3	28.2	28.3	22.7	40.9	35.4

Source: National Family Health Survey (NFHS-3), 2005-06, India, IIPS, Volume I, p.302.

Table 5.10

Prevalence of Anaemia in Women and Men by State and All India, 2005-06

(Percentage of women and men age 15-49 with anaemia)

State/All India	*Mild Anaemia*		*Moderate Anaemia*		*Severe Anaemia*		*Any Anaemia*	
	Male	*Female*	*Male*	*Female*	*Male*	*Female*	*Male*	*Female*
Manipur	6.8	30.1	4.2	5.1	0.4	0.5	11.4	35.7
India	13.0	38.6	9.9	15.0	1.3	1.8	24.2	55.3

Source: National Family Health Survey (NFHS-3), 2005-06, India, IIPS, Volume I, p.313.

Manipur is better than the national scenario (Table 5.10).

Political Indicators

Women's political participation is one of the important issues in the context of empowerment.

Political empowerment refers to the equitable representation of women in decision-making structures, both formal and informal, and their voice in the formulation of policies affecting their societies. Women in Manipur are poorly represented in the lower levels of government, they are rarer still in the upper echelons of decision-making.

Women's Participation in Decision-making

Participation in decision-making process is significant from different angles. Some of the important ones are the potential to remove involuntary exploitation and the scope for creating outcomes that constitute movement towards establishment of gender equity. This significance is particularly so in a society like Manipur's where traditional and informal sector employment predominates. Here, as seen from Table 5.11, we can say that the situation prevailing in Manipur is not only far better than the national scenario but also good.

Table 5.11

Percentage of Currently Married Women Taking Decisions either by Themselves or Jointly with their Husband, 2005-2006

Manipur/ All India	*Own Health Care*	*Making major House-hold Purch-ases*	*Making purch-ases for daily house-hold needs*	*Visits to her family or rela-tives*	*Per centage who part-icipate in all the four decisions*	*Per centage who parti-cipate in none of the four decisions*
Manipur	87.4	81.4	85.2	86.0	69.4	3.4
All-India	62.2	52.9	60.1	60.5	36.7	20.5

Source: *National Family Health Su. vey (NFHS-3), 2005-06*, India, IIPS, Volume I, p.467.

Domestic Violence

Violence against women is a manifestation of the historically unequal power relations between men and women, which led to domination over and discrimination against women by men. This can happen both at the intra-household and the societal level. The reality and threat of violence is a hindrance in a woman's life and limits her ability to participate and contribute fully to the society. It also adversely impact upon the health of women too.

The 1993 UN General Assembly Declaration on the Elimination of Violence against Women defined it as "any act of gender-based violence that results in, or is likely to result in, physical, sexual or psychological harm or suffering to women, including threats of such acts, coercion or arbitrary deprivation of liberty, whether occurring in public or private life." This includes:

- Intra-household violence – physical, sexual and psychological violence occurring in the family, like battering, sexual abuse of female children, and dowry-related violence. This is generally known as domestic violence.
- Social violence – physical, sexual and psychological violence occurring within the general community, like rape, sexual abuse, sexual harassment and intimidation at work, in educational institutions and elsewhere, trafficking in women, and forced prostitution.
- State sponsored violence – physical, sexual and psychological violence perpetrated or condoned by the State wherever it occurs.

Whereas it is controversial and involves wider agreement among the general population in the case of the last two categories of violence, it is equally difficult to establish prevalence of violence at the domestic level in the absence of disclosure by the victims.

Table 5.12
Per centage of Ever-Married Women age 15-49 who have Experienced Different Types of Violence Committed by their Husband* by State and All-India, 2005-2006

(Percentage who have experienced)

State/ All-India	*Emotional Violence*	*Physical Violence*	*Sexual Violence*	*Physical or sexual Violence*	*Emotional or Physical or Sexual Violence*
Manipur	13.9	40.7	14.0	43.8	46.2
All-India	15.8	35.1	10.0	37.2	39.2

Source: *National Family Health Survey (NFHS-3), 2005-06*, India, IIPS, Volume I, p.519.

* Husband refers to the current husband for currently married women and the most recent husband for widowed, divorced, separated, or deserted women.

A picture of the domestic violence perpetrated by husbands is available from the National Family Health Survey. Here the data portray a very paradoxical picture. As seen from Table 5.12, the domestic violence rates are higher in Manipur than the National average in all the five indicators for which we have information. This picture drastically contradicts the general perception of status of women relatively higher in Manipur.

Index

■■■